Love Letters
to Navigate the
Grief Journey

Andrew Rienstra

ISBN 978-1-63903-464-2 (paperback)
ISBN 978-1-63903-465-9 (digital)

Christian Faith Publishing, Inc.
832 Park Avenue
Meadville, PA 16335
www.christianfaithpublishing.com

Printed in the United States of America

Contents

Introduction

"Why are you writing letters to your deceased wife?" This is a question a number of people have asked me when I mentioned I was doing so. After all, she is no longer alive and unable to respond. It is also a question I have repeatedly asked myself as I experience both the pain and joy of doing so. It all began with the suggestion of a friend who told me it would be a special way to experience and share my grief. The more I reflected, the more I liked the suggestion. It became apparent that there were two reasons to do so.

First, I needed some grief therapy. Due to my nature, I was aware I would be reluctant to seek it. Perhaps writing out my feelings in letters would be a form of therapy. Mae and I always had vibrant, lively, and energizing conversations about all manner of subjects; and although we often had opposing views, we talked with an attitude where both were very ready to learn from the other, even though at times we wanted to persuade. On our first date, we talked for hours, and ever since, there was never a lack of conversation. Our marriage survived its many scuffles because we kept talking and communicating. We always enjoyed our long car trips. We would find a myriad of reasons to converse. It was either something we saw along the road, a remark by someone on the radio, or a memory that came to mind in the spur of the moment. We thoroughly enjoyed talking to each other. That is the toughest part of my loss. I miss our conversations the most! I wanted so much to continue to talk with her even though she was not physically present. So I decided to write and figured it would be a challenge to help me work through my grieving. I'm sure many of the conversations may not be interesting to others, but I hope some of them ignite thoughts that will be helpful to others on their grief journey.

I wanted to tell her about daily experiences, things that were on my mind because of happenings in our family or in the world, and especially my feelings of loneliness. She generally listened attentively to what I had to say, often with the intention of affirming and at other times to challenge me to think beyond where I was at the moment. In writing, I came to feel that she was listening, helping me feel her spiritual aliveness. Since I never did go for any formal grief therapy, the writing has served that purpose.

The second reason was the awareness that a number of others who had lost their spouse showed a great interest in how I was coping. I also was interested in hearing from them. I wanted to hear their story. I found great support in reading books others had written. I felt I had a message to share that would be equally of interest and hopefully helpful to those crossing over the deep chasm of grief.

It is my desire to be open and honest about feelings. With some men, there is a reluctance to share feelings, especially of physical and emotional intimacy. We tend to hide and bury such feelings. I want to coax openness! Hopefully these letters can help promote that.

I feel deeply the pain of those who have lost loved ones. The reason I chose ministry as a profession goes back to high school days when my best friend at that time was killed in a tragic train car accident. It had a major impact on the small town in which we lived. The subsequent response to grief on the part of so many moved me to want to be a grief helper, a person who could help others find hope and encouragement. It became my call to ministry. My chief focus as a pastor and preacher has been to be a hope builder. May these letters also serve that purpose.

You played the piano so beautifully. It was one of your gifts you shared that attracted me. This is a special picture of us both at the piano on a evening you would be playing for guests.

My Decision to Write You!

Dear Mae,

Mark Aukema, our sister-in-law Carol's father, had dinner with Rusty, Carol, Jeanne, and myself recently. Among other things, Mark and I discussed how we felt having lost the love of our life. He is ninety-four and was married seventy years to Betty. She died a couple years ago. I was interested in how he was surviving without her. Among some of the interesting things he related was finding a stash of letters they had written to each other during their courtship. One of his daughters discovered them in Betty's hope chest. He doesn't ever remember seeing them in the seventy years of their marriage. He related how he is now opening one each evening and reflecting on all the thoughts and memories that come to mind as he lies in bed before falling asleep.

As I listened, I was doubtful that would work for me at bedtime, but I felt a sadness that you and I had not preserved our courtship letters. You remember, I am sure, that we burned them one day shortly after we moved into our first real home on Richards-Gebaur Air Force Base. You were pregnant and said you didn't want your children to ever find those letters in which we expressed so many intimate feelings. I can't help but think you felt this way due to the fact you and your inquisitive single aunts all lived in the same house, and you felt they often attempted to discover things you desired to be kept secret. You always suspected that they read stuff you wanted to keep secret, so you sort of developed a pattern of secrecy about things you wrote, especially what you wrote to me at that time.

Anyway, you suggested we burn them, and as I recall it was more than a suggestion. You were quite determined to do it, and I agreed even though I thought at that time it was unnecessary. I especially feel that way today. I wish I was able to read some of those letters now that you are gone. It has moved me to make this decision. I am going to write you a whole new set of letters, and they will not be hidden. They will be shared with all who may be interested and will reflect many of the feelings that have overwhelmed me since your sudden departure.

I need to thank Rich Bierwas for the idea (pastor of the Ho Ho Kus Reformed church, whom I mentored during his initial years in the pastorate). I had lunch with him recently and indicated my desire to write a book about what it is like to live with great grief. A couple days later, he wrote a "thank you" note and suggested I do so by way of letters to you. I liked the idea and will write a series of them. When, and of course if, you are able to read them, I know you won't want them destroyed. You have grown so much since those early days of innocence and have become wonderfully open about who you are. You encouraged me to be more open and challenged so many others to be as well. When we kissed goodbye that last morning, we were not finished with our open sharing, so here goes from me. I just wish I could listen to your response, until some greater moment.

Love you, honey.

Andrew

The Day You Were Killed

Dear Mae,

I often wonder how you experienced the end of your life. Did you feel the impact of the collision? Was there a moment of awareness, or was your life over like the snap of a finger, one short breath? I will never know. I wish I could because you were always so fascinated about those stories of after-life experiences, how people died and what happened next. I would like to hear your description of your first after-death moment. That can't happen, but at least I can tell you about my first bit of awareness after finding out you were dead.

I remember how difficult the weekend had been for me. I wasn't feeling well, and you were ever concerned about my health. You were anxious about my non-Hodgkin's lymphoma returning, so you were very determined that I not attend church or Jerry Walborn's retirement party on that Sunday. You wanted me to stay home and "just rest." You were repeatedly telling me that my main purpose in life at that time was to get fully healed. In bed that night, we discussed our plans for the next day, and you tried to convince me that you should go along to visit the doctor for my normal six-month checkup. Since you had a date to take pictures of alpacas near Nazareth, Pennsylvania, with the women from your photo class, I felt I could easily go alone. We went to sleep not having resolved the issue. When we awoke in the morning, you were still insisting on going along. After more discussion, I convinced you I could go by myself; and you relented, gathered your cameras, and left about an hour before I went to the doctor. Ever since then, I have become less interested in getting people to change their minds.

The appointment turned out even better than expected. He checked all my vitals and blood test results, and we talked some about golf and life in general. He said that if his blood work was as good as mine at age eighty, he would be delighted. He encouraged me to continue doing what I was doing and enjoy. In a rather extended conversation for a doctor's visit, he told me about his cousin who had recently been diagnosed with pancreatic cancer. He made the remark that, in many ways, "life is a crap shoot." We never know what is around the corner! I agreed, and we parted with pleasantries. I could not wait to get home and let you know the good news. I wanted to convince you that most of your concern was unwarranted. I was in excellent health, just had a normal bad week. I was eager to bust you a bit about being so overly cautious all the time about my condition.

As I waited, you didn't come home. You had promised that we would have lunch together and then go to Shawnee and play some golf. I even put a cup of soup in the microwave because I was getting hungry and didn't feel like waiting any longer. At that moment, I noticed a state police car turning into our driveway. I wondered why they were there and then remembered there was a person the police were tracking down in that part of Pennsylvania. He had killed a police officer at their barracks a week or so previously, and they hadn't found him. He was considered dangerous, and they were anxious to bring him into custody.

Graciously, I welcomed two young officers, a male and female, into our living room and beckoned them to take a seat. Both seemed quite somber, but I figured this is how young officers are trained to meet the public under such circumstances. We chatted for a few moments. I don't recall about what. Then the young lady, who was probably about twenty-three years of age, asked me if I had heard about the accident on Route 209. When I said no, she responded by saying, rather matter-of-factly as I can remember now, "Your wife was killed." She then informed me how the accident had happened. She told me that while you were stopped at the red light on Route 209 and Shafers Schoolhouse Road, a semi crashed into your rear end; and as a result, you were killed and your friend in the back seat was seriously injured and flown by helicopter to Leigh Hospital (she died a couple hours later). The two women in the front were seriously injured.

I must have experienced serious shock. I really can't remember the feeling. If anything, I probably felt numb! All I know is that I stood up and said nothing for a couple moments, just looked at them, and then started to tell of an experience from my early days as an Air Force Chaplain stationed at Richards-Gebaur AFB in Missouri where we had our first home. You would remember what happened. It was the crash of the Air Force cargo plane at the base when eight airmen were killed, all reservists living in the nearby Kansas City area. They had been recalled for the Berlin crisis in 1960. As far as I can remember, that is the first time that incident appeared in my memory since shortly after it happened. It was so chaotic; I must have blocked it out completely for years.

The plane had taken off from the base with equipment and a crew of eight when it encountered engine trouble and needed to return. At that time, the Catholic chaplain and I, the Protestant, were called to the flight line, as regularly occurred when there was an emergency. A red "crash phone" located in the chapel alerted us. We hurried to our assigned place and watched as this plane with a crippled engine glided toward the prepared runway with all kinds of emergency equipment and personnel ready to respond. The plane never reached the runway. It crashed short, causing a huge explosion and fire. All personnel on board were killed.

After the fire was extinguished enough so that fire personnel and others could move about the wreckage, the Catholic chaplain said that he had to administer last rites to the human remains. He asked me to accompany him. Since there was still some smoke and smoldering parts, we were dressed in asbestos suits and accompanied by fire personnel with extinguishers. We found nothing but body parts. The fire had pretty well destroyed everything else. My Catholic friend did his part, and after we discovered the names and records of those killed, we found out that all eight were protestant. This meant that I was the chaplain who would accompany the reserve unit commander to notify the families. I wonder if you remember how anxious I was about that assignment. How was I going to do that? I was just twenty-five years old, and it was my first death notification! I related that story to these young police officers and added, "I know well what it is like to be in your place right now. I have done it many other times since. Now I know how it feels to be the person being informed."

My story must have shocked them a bit. It was obvious they were not well prepared for their task. They acted quite anxious, offered to get some medical help if needed; but when I said that I could carry on and I needed to inform family, they rather quickly departed. Looking back, I don't know how I survived the day. The first person I called was my brother, John. I needed to tell somebody in the family, but not the girls. Next, I called Pastor Kathleen (Edwards Chase). I asked her to inform Karen, and she willingly volunteered to tell Candice as well. Then I called Gerry so he could tell Richelle. I also called your family. I can't fully recall, but I think I called your brother-in-law Jim and asked him to inform everyone. It is very confusing for me to try to remember the sequence of everything.

Neighbors evidently heard it on news outlets. It was a big accident; everyone heard about it quickly and began to stop over. Most of that day remains fuzzy, except for Chris McClosky taking me to the scene of the accident. This was early evening, and the intersection was still closed and roped off. He also took me to the police station to pick up your belongings. Your favorite red camera was smashed to bits. I still have your little camera, and Richelle eventually got your good camera and lens. I stayed busy all day and must have been running on adrenaline. Neighbors invited me to come for supper, and some also brought food. I told them to hold off on the food because I just was not hungry. Many people called on the phone once they heard. I can't remember who, except I know I talked with all our daughters. I don't remember what we said to each other. I think I just listened to them cry. I couldn't cry. Richelle immediately got on a flight for Newark, and Karen waited for her to get there, and then they both came to be with me the next day. I told Karen to stay with her family the first night. She needed to be with Bruce and her kids more than I needed her. I could make it alone.

One call I remember was from Mary Peterson. She had heard from Rusty and Carol. Talking with her helped me get to sleep, I think. Having just lost Ron recently and also being a counselor, she listened and said the right things to respond to my pain. I really can't remember what we talked about, but it was long and helpful. It was surely the worst day of my life. I get terrible feelings writing about it. This is all I am going to write for now. I will pick up on what happened, succeeding days, and also the wonderful celebration of your life we staged.

Love you so much, honey! I so wish I could talk with you right now about the terror of that day.

Love you.

Andrew

The Days Between Death and Life Celebration

Hi, honey,

We called each other "honey" a lot, didn't we? All our friends remind me often that you called me that, but when you were upset with me or wanted to stress something, you called me Andrew, but never Andy. I liked that others knew me as Andy. They even formally addressed me as the Rev. Dr. Andy. But my given name is Andrew, and you liked it and called me that, and I liked it as well.

Let me get to some more stuff about the days that followed your death. You died on October 13, 2014, Columbus Day. On the 26th of October, we had a wonderful celebration of your life at the church in Pompton Plains. I call it wonderful because it was. It was inspirational. It was well-planned; and it moved us all to tears of joy, as well as sorrow, as we reflected on the many ways you touched our lives. More about that later, but now let me share some of what I can remember about the time between the day of your death and that day.

Richelle took the red-eye from Los Angeles and arrived early in the morning. Later that morning, she and Karen came to Pennsylvania to be with me. The moment they walked in the house, they began to scream and cry like little kids. You remember how they screamed when they were upset? Well, this was ten times more earsplitting, just witnessing the place where they always expected to see you set them off, and me too. Until that moment, I had not cried. But then

I let it all hang out, and I haven't stopped since. Of course, not in the manner of the first cry, but my tears do not go away. The least little thought can open the tear ducts.

Once we curtailed the heavy weeping, we began to discuss the duties we had to accomplish and how we were going to celebrate your life. The next few days, we did a host of things together. We made arrangements with a funeral home in Stroudsburg where your body had been taken and informed them to contact Scanlan's in Pompton Plains. Before they released your body, we had the opportunity to view and bid you our final farewells. Karen and I did, but Richelle didn't want to look at your lifeless body. She wanted to remember you as the lively mother you were. When Karen and I looked at you, it was very sad. Fortunately, your body did not suffer much physical damage. Undoubtedly, it was the impact of the collision that caused brain damage and death. Your body was not damaged. They had done an autopsy, required by law when such an accident occurs, so it took a couple days before we could see you. We didn't remain long. Karen gave you a kiss and cried. I hugged, kissed you, also with a lot of tears, and we left. Not the most pleasant way to experience our last look at you, but what I remember was the beauty you projected through every part of your body and person. I still think of how many of my male golf friends used to bust me about my trophy wife. They wondered how this very normal looking guy could have caught such a beauty. I still keep pictures of you on my desktop computer screen and thank God daily that I was so fortunate. Although I was proud of your physical beauty, it was your inner beauty that was there for all to see.

Once your body arrived at Scanlan's, we met with members of their staff. They were most helpful and encouraging, as I had always found them to be, during the many funerals I conducted with them over the twenty-one years in Pompton Plains. They gave us a nice discount and made all the arrangements for your cremation and interment. We also met with Pastor Kathleen to plan the funeral. We chose five women to reflect on your life: your friends Bev and Midge, your nieces Janelle and Rachael, and sister-in-law Marti. The choir committed to sing, and Kathleen was willing to do the eulogy and homily. I also made plans to say something and thank everyone for being part of the service and supporting our family during those difficult days.

We also had to make plans for family members and friends who were coming in from out of the area. Fortunately, a couple of our friends helped out with this. The Kirkwoods made rooms available in the Shawnee Inn, and Steve Holmes arranged for condos in Wyndham rentals in the Shawnee community. Since the people of Pompton Plains anticipated a large turnout for the service on Sunday afternoon, Rotary got involved. They parked cars and made sure there were sufficient spaces. You would have been proud of all those friends in the community who couldn't do enough to make that day the best it could be, giving honor to you for all you meant to them. I hope, in some way, in God's great new adventure, you had the opportunity to witness the wonder of that day and the love people expressed for you.

Good night for now. I miss those hugs before we fell off to sleep. I guess you don't miss my snoring!

Love and kisses,
Andrew

The Funeral

Hon,

I want to tell you about the funeral, or better, the celebration of your life. It was an event like no one could anticipate. All the grandkids and our kids and their spouses were able to be present. Gerry and Alex, Richard and Miranda came in from California; and Joshua, Garrett, and Karlee were also present. Your sisters Lois and Dot, brother, Leon, and Donna and Jim Meyer were also able to come. My brothers, John and Rusty, sister, Jeanne and Carol and Marti, were also with us. All the immediate family members, plus nephews Chad, Luke, and Jon-Jon, were there. It was a grand gathering! Too bad it takes death to bring us all together. The evening before the funeral, we were able to gather at the Shawnee Inn for dinner. We enjoyed some of the best food ever at Shawnee. Dave and Bev had also arrived and were able to be at the dinner. The only family member absent was Candice, but she did come to the funeral. Richelle and Gerry and the kids stayed with me. The rest of our families stayed in the rooms and condos in Shawnee. It all worked out better than I could anticipate, believe me. I was very anxious about how we would provide for all guests and relatives and enjoy some time to share with each other.

The life celebration was at the church at 2:00 p.m. on Sunday, the 26th of October. It was, without a doubt, the most joyful celebration of someone's life I have ever witnessed. Of course, I am very prejudiced. To begin, the church and friendship hall were filled to capacity. People had to be turned away, and fortunately the entire celebration was livestreamed so people who couldn't get in could witness it. And many of our friends who live in other parts of the country were able to be present on their computers. They had a big screen up in friendship hall for those who had to sit there because the sanctuary was packed full.

The service lasted for almost two hours, but no one complained about the length. They all commented on how each participant was so alive with wonderful stories of your life and how you had influenced them. The choir sang. John and Amy Hellyer sang. Kathleen had a wonderful homily. I concluded the service with a word of thanks and a challenge to see your death not as the end of something but the beginning of something new for you and all of us. I was challenged to share those thoughts because of a picture Bonnie Holmes sent from China. Steve had a business trip there the week you died, and Bonnie went along. One of her kids shared on her phone the news of your death. When she heard about it, she took a walk and saw a fountain with a rainbow behind it. She snapped the picture and sent it to me with the words that whenever she sees a rainbow, she will think of you. That got me thinking about the biblical image of the rainbow, how it symbolized new beginnings and how I especially needed to see your death as a new beginning for both of us. I try to keep that image alive in my mind as often as possible. Some days, I feel like giving up and not caring about much of anything. Some nights, I go to bed with the hope that I won't awake the next morning. Overall, however, I try to keep the metaphor of the rainbow alive and that helps me keep on keeping on.

After the funeral, we all gathered at Karen and Bruce's place to share beverages and goodies. It was a good time to simply be with our combined families. Parting was difficult when the evening came to an end. Rusty and Carol and Jeanne left early the next morning and on their way through Pennsylvania, ran into a deer. Their car was totaled, but no one was injured. They were frightened but able to rent a car and get home that same day. It was especially difficult to bid Richelle and her family farewell. Richelle was a great strength for me between your death and the funeral. She stayed with me, and although Karen was also of help, she had to go home to stay with her family. Candice did come to the funeral and did greet people, but tired before we left the church, and Gerry took her home early. In all, it was one of the most memorable days of my life, and in retrospect, a day of great joy and sadness mixed together in a strange blend of emotions.

Hugs and kisses, will write again soon!

Andrew

After the Funeral

Hi, Mae,

Everyone had gone home, and now I was all alone and acutely realized the necessity to carve out a new life. Fortunately, we made some very good friends in our neighborhood, the Shawnee Church and Shawnee Country Club. Many people have taken a special interest in me being alone. They have made special effort to ensure I know they are there and available to help. I have kept up my usual two or three-day golf matches each week, and all the guys are very alert to my feelings, almost too much so at times. I regularly attend church at Shawnee, and everyone reaches out beyond my expectation. The Kirkwoods have been especially supportive. Each Sunday evening, they have dinner at their home with family and friends and regularly invite me. We always have interesting and invigorating conversations. It helps me forget some of the lonely feelings.

Your Memorial Stone attracts my frequent visits. I utter prayers of gratitude and shed some tears as I attempt to sense your presence.

I have continued my work as a retiree chaplain. For a while, I considered retiring, but after conversations with some of our friends, I decided it is good to have some regular responsibilities. It motivates me to keep in contact with the various people we have visited. It is also enjoyable to interact with them and engage in discussions about their lives which moves me out of myself and feelings of "pity me." I tend to do that—sit out in the front yard, swing with a glass of wine, feeling all alone and almost without purpose. I get the feeling that life just won't be any fun anymore without you. I have done some preaching but have turned down most requests. I do a few, especially to keep my mind alert and become energized by the challenge of meeting and speaking with people about things that really matter.

I mentioned that Mary Peterson called the day you died, and I have kept in phone contact with her regularly. She was very helpful, having lost Ron and having been trained to do counseling. She helps me see how I need to work through the emptiness of living without you. It is also helpful that we were such good friends while they lived in New Jersey. We share many great memories and have good laughs. We especially remember a very cold day being on a ski lift together, and she said, "Andy, hell is going to be cold." Those humorous memories provide a lightness I need. My family also keeps in touch: Jeanne, John, and Marti and Rusty and Carol. Of course, Richelle calls regularly. I know all that will change, and I must carve out a more independent life.

At times in the past, when I spoke with people who have lost a close family member, I would suggest a grief group or at least a professional counselor, but I don't feel a desire for it at this time. I think if our roles were reversed, you would have found some group to help you as soon as possible. You did that when we first discovered mental illness with Candice, and it was very helpful. I guess because of all the training and experience I have had in people-helping skills, I am reluctant to reach out for help. Maybe I will need to do differently in the future.

I will write again soon! I will never cease feeling the great love I have for you.

Andrew

Back to the Pulpit

Morning, hon.

I wish I could wake up and find you in bed next to me. Some mornings, I do wake up thinking you are there and move cautiously not to wake you. Then the awful truth strikes. You are not there and never will be. I do remember there were times when you could be a little grumpy if I woke you. Some of the feelings I get now are about how I often did not take your feelings into consideration. I would wake early to get to the "Y" by six, make more noise than necessary, and interrupt your sleep; and when you complained about it, I came back with some smart remark about how you would enjoy the day more if you started earlier. I would never say that to you now!

What I do want to tell you about today is my preaching experience since your death. You were always such an affirming voice about my preaching. You gave me confidence by your presence in the pew and the smile on your face. I knew you were listening, and if you thought anything was not right about what I said, you would approach me with a positive reaction and comment. About a half year after you died, Kathleen was given a sabbatical for a month to have some time by herself and sort out some issues in her life. Since it was in May and the season of the year for confirmation and other concluding events in the church year, she approached me about filling the pulpit for the four Sundays she was gone. I hesitated for over a week to give her a reply. I hadn't preached since the time of your death and was not sure if I wanted to preach at all anymore. After some praying and consultation with friends, I decided to do it. I put together four different sermons, expressing much of my feelings about God and life following your death.

Although I did relate to the needs of the congregation (i.e., confirmation, baptism, etc., at that time), I shared thoughts on tears and loneliness, feelings of loss and grief, and stories of my recent experiences. The first Sunday was very difficult doing both services, but after the second Sunday it almost seemed like I was back where I had been over ten years previous. I enjoyed it very much and determined that I would do some more preaching upon request in various places. The one thing I missed most was being able to exchange ideas with you, get your feedback, and discuss as we did so often. You have always had the right insight about how things were said and how they affected people's attitudes and feelings. You often served as a corrective to help me clarify a thought without unnecessarily offending the people to whom I was speaking. I feel somewhat less confident not seeing you out in the audience with your radiant smile.

Kisses and hugs.

"It was tough getting back in the
pulpit and not seeing your radiant
face among the worshipers."

Moving Back to New Jersey

Good morning, Mae!

I need to wake in the morning and know that, in some fashion, I can still communicate with you. So I enjoy writing these letters. Today I want to share with you my decision to move back to New Jersey. Although I was golfing regularly with the group of guys and was able to spend a couple months of my first winter without you in Florida, I felt the need for some female companionship. I hadn't had either lunch or dinner with a female and felt the need to do so. I was thinking about whom I might invite to enjoy dinner together. Someone we both know from Pompton Plains came to mind—Linda Rooney. She had lost her husband Tom some years earlier, and I figured we would have something in common to share. She also struck me as having a very caring personality, a ready mind, and an attractive appearance. I invited her to share dinner at the Stroudsmoor Inn for the Friday night seafood buffet. She accepted, and we enjoyed sharing thoughts about our pain in having lost our loving spouses.

Following that evening, we kept in touch; and in a subsequent conversation, she suggested that I consider moving back to New Jersey, being closer to our daughters, Candice and Karen. She also realized, as you did, that driving up and down Mt. Nebo Road was quite risky in the winter. She took the initiative to set up an appointment with a realtor at a condominium complex where her friends had recently purchased. Although I hadn't considered moving at that time, I thought it would be better for all if I was nearer both the girls.

On a Thursday, a couple weeks later, we met for lunch at a nearby Olive Garden and then met the realtor. I think you would have appreciated the realtor. She was friendly and engaging and took us to see the models. Stepping into the first model, which opened into the kitchen, I thought of you and how you would like the lay-out. There was just something about it that told me you would love it. After looking at a couple more models, we sat and talked. She said that since the company wanted to complete construction as soon as possible, they were making a special offer on Sunday. If I would return on Sunday and was able to close by November 30 (it was sometime near the end of October), she could give me a substantial discount.

Although I had not seriously thought about selling and buying a new place and moving, I was very attracted by the complex and models. I sort of liked a large one-bedroom unit which had an extra little study room. It had 1 and 1/2 baths. I thought it was just right for me. I could dispose of a lot of our stuff and start a new life in a new place. Arriving home that night, I called Karen and asked if she would go with me on Sunday to look at the units and listen to the offers. She was very willing, and we met at the realtor's office about 10:00 a.m. I skipped church that day. Karen was very impressed by the units and the amenities that were part of the complex. There is an indoor pool, a small gym, an outdoor pool, all part of a beautifully designed clubhouse. There are also other rooms in the clubhouse: a large meeting room, a billiards room, a room for making pottery, a mini library, a room for dance lessons and yoga, and a boardroom. Decorations and furnishings are exquisite.

When we sat with the realtor to talk about purchase, she revealed that she could give a 50,000-dollar discount. I was ready to sign up immediately for the one-bedroom unit, but Karen was not. She figured I should have the two-bedroom, which was located in the building overlooking the outdoor pool. Her reasoning was that it would give more space to have overnight guests and also provide for the time when I might need to have live-in help. You were often surprised by my willingness to make quick decisions and how often they were right. I did this time as well and am convinced it was another right decision. I accepted the offer. I knew it was the right place to live at that time, and I could work it out financially. It is five minutes off Route 80, forty-five minutes from our home in Pennsylvania, about thirty minutes from Pompton Plains, a little over forty minutes from Karen and Bruce, and right next to Picatinny Arsenal. If you remember the back gate we used when we went golfing, the complex is on that street, Mount Hope Road. Additionally, Rockaway Mall is just on the other side of Rt. 80, as well as Costco. I signed the papers and bought the unit and am very happy I did.

They always say one should never do anything, like move, until at least a year after the time of loss. So it was just over a year, and I was going to make this big change. I was concerned about selling our home. I knew I would never get out what we put in it, especially with the third bedroom added and the generator. We had also replaced the roof and the heat/AC unit, but then we had enjoyed living there for fifteen years. A few days after signing the contract, I contacted Frank Scangarella to serve as a lawyer. He was impressed with the complex and affirmed me in making the purchase. With a sense of confidence that I had done well, I began to contact realtors. Three of them came in to give estimates; and there was a high, low, and medium range. Surprisingly, there was a $50,000 difference between low and high. I can't help but think the high estimate was made with the hope of getting the listing and then in the future making excuses about the market because it wasn't selling for the list price. Anyway, a surprise developed, and I didn't have to deal with realtors.

Roland Petite called and requested me to speak at the Pastoral Care Day for Chilton hospital. This is an annual event at which clergy and pastoral-care givers are invited to attend. Roland wanted me to speak about how the pastoral-care department began at Chilton. I agreed, and the date was your birthday—October 30. In the course of the speech, I mentioned that I was returning to live in New Jersey. Later at lunch, Tom Bartha from Pompton Lakes asked if I was selling my house. When I said yes, he asked if he and Mary could come to take a look. He was anticipating retirement and had been looking at homes in Pennsylvania. We set a date and time for their visit. Once they arrived and took a look at the house and neighborhood, they quickly decided they wanted to buy. Not only the house, but they also agreed to buy much of our furniture and all the stuff we had outside: the swing set, mower, snow blower, and everything stored in the garage and on the deck.

The price I asked was the middle estimate, and Tom and Mary were not only agreeable but added extra dollars for all the furniture and equipment. We took a few weeks to complete the closing. We had to get lawyers, an inspection, and a few other things accomplished, which you would have done so well. I surely missed your real estate expertise! You would be happy to know that the inspectors determined everything to be in great shape. One of them even said, "I would be willing to buy this place. Everything is excellent." The date for closing was set to occur before the end of the year to minimize tax-related factors. I had the same attorney I used for the wrongful death suit made against the trucking company and trucker who caused your accident. He was referred by a friend and served well. The closing took just a matter of minutes, and afterward, Tom and Mary met me at the house so we could share some other things about which we hadn't talked previously, like the grinder pump light and how to program the garage door into their car, etc.

So much for now! Love you much!

"Honey, you would love this pool which can be seen as is from my third floor condo."

The Move

"Without the assistance of Bruce and Karen I would never
have been able make the move. So grateful for their help.

Dear Mae,

The move from our home to the new condo took place the day
before my eighty-first birthday. I used the same moving company we
did moving to Sunrise Village in 2004, Most Outstanding Movers,
Don Budd, who also moved us to Pennsylvania. They did a great job,
packed everything the day before, and completed the move the following day. Bruce and Karen's help was exceptional. If it weren't for
them, I never could have done it. We had planned the move at that
time because Bruce would not be working and could give full effort.

He took most of the stuff that wasn't sold, couldn't be put into the condo, and I didn't need anymore.

Because the beds and most of the bedroom furniture were sold to the Barthas, I purchased a new bed, a pullout sofa couch, and a recliner. They were all in place when the mover arrived with what was taken from Pennsylvania. That first night was very strange, living in a new home and without you. I took a picture to share on Facebook, sitting in the recliner in the living room, looking at the temporary window treatments Karen had hung. I shed both tears of joy and sorrow because I was happy to be in this new safe and beautiful place and thought of how much you would have enjoyed being there with me and how much you were missed. I made the purchase of the condo primarily because I needed it, but additionally because I knew it was the kind of living space you would have enjoyed as well.

Through the whole moving process, my mind kept bringing up things you would be saying to the movers, to Karen and Bruce, and myself about how to handle things and where you would want them eventually placed. It brought me back to the time you helped Gerry and Richelle move and Gerry's friends referred to you as the "commandant." Even though you weren't physically present, you were there in our awareness of how you functioned under such circumstances. Your presence and spirit ever remain alive, and it particularly did that day. We finished the move with dinner provided by Carolyn Connerton. She lives in the adjacent complex called Fox Hills. If you recall, we scouted out that complex when we were looking for a place to purchase for retirement. It was all very nice, but at that time, you did not want a condo. You wanted a house which eventually brought us to Pennsylvania. My complex is in the back of Fox Hills, a whole different community, and is called Greenbriar at Fox Ridge. There are numerous fox roaming the area, and I guess that accounts for the name.

The next day, we celebrated my birthday with Karen and Bruce, helping to get everything in place. Pictures were hung, dishes put into the various cabinets, along with pots and pans. I don't remember much from the birthday celebration but realize that Karen provided me with many of the things necessary for a new apartment. Karen has much of the energy and creativity you possessed, and it was so nice to have her there, making the place very livable. The window treatments she hung could have stayed up far longer than they did since they were very attractive. Karen eventually assisted in securing permanent treatments which were some of the most expensive items in decorating the place. It was also wonderful to have a caring son-in-law as strong and sensitive as Bruce. They really made the move a mostly enjoyable experience. I just wish you had been in on it. I remember that a couple weeks before your accident, you had reminded me of a promise I made that we would live in Pennsylvania for ten years and then move closer to the girls. You would have loved this move.

In addition to Bruce and Karen's help getting the condo ready for living, I employed George Douglas to build a computer desk in the corner of my bedroom, hang the TVs and the heavier pictures. The unit was painted before the move. I thought it's best to do it that way, and then it would not be such a difficult task to paint with all the furniture in place. Others in the building waited, and it proved to be more costly and more trouble. George also put up some fixtures in the bathrooms to hang towels and washcloths and hung some racks in the closets. Subsequently, I contacted a closet company to install the latest shelves, drawers, and clothes racks in all four of them. One has become partly a cupboard and outdoor-coat closet. The desk turned out to be magnificent. It is at a perfect height, has three nice-size drawers, and plenty of space for things needed to be stored on top. It's perfect!

I wish you could stop in and see the place, and we could enjoy sleeping in the special new bed together. I bought the best we could find. Bruce and Karen helped me choose it, and we were able to get it at a discount through one of Bruce's friends. It can be moved in a myriad of positions and has a number of ways to provide vibration. You would love it!

I love you!

Andrew

Survival Benefits

Good morning, darling! How are we doing with money? It was a question often on your mind. You were a thrifty spouse and took pride in your bargain hunting. I remember well how you took over the checkbook in our first year of marriage because you were unhappy with my spending and accounting for where money was spent. Your friend Pat Hellyer would always call you "bargain basement Mazy." Since we had figured I would precede you to the grave, our finances were set up in a way that the benefits from my Air Force pension and other smaller pensions from the churches would be able to support you, along with other investments we had made. Of course, it didn't work that way, but ironically it worked well for me and the girls. I call it bittersweet money, the kind I would just as soon not have received, but it serves well.

Because of the nature of the accident and the fact that the truck driver was distracted by his cell phone, or whatever, and was speeding when he smashed into the rear end of the car, all involved were interested in discovering the possible insurance benefits. One of our friends from Shawnee Church gave me a suggestion of a lawyer who might be helpful. I contacted him and arranged an appointment for Richelle and myself to meet. We were pleased with his manner and attitude, and he was willing to take on the case. He suggested a "wrongful death claim" against the trucking company and driver due to the obvious negligence. It was a surprise that lawyers doing that kind of work get one third of everything they recover, seemed large but discovered that is the going rate.

He told us that it would undoubtedly take years for everything to be settled, and we should not expect any pay out in the near future, especially if it goes to a trial by jury. He also assured us that given the facts of the accident, it was rather certain that we would receive some compensation. He did indicate that because of your age at death, we should not expect a large sum. The size of payouts is determined by the monetary value of the deceased to the family. Since you were seventy-six at that time and no longer employed, your monetary value was quite limited. We did talk about emotional value, which we indicated was significant, especially because of the care you provided Candice on disability. After he got all the information he desired, he gave a list of things and information we had to furnish for him to get busy. I signed the contract and left for home. It was most depressing. Here I had lost the most important person in my life, and my daughter's mother, and we are talking about her monetary value. This was not the way I wanted to measure your value. How could your significance for us be measured in dollars and cents, be they big bucks or small! Yet that is the way our culture and economic system works, and we would be foolish not to work through it with this lawyer. The other families involved also hired lawyers, all different.

Our lawyer kept in touch regularly. Whenever he had something to report, he called or e-mailed, and I felt he was working as diligently and as quickly as he could to bring a resolution. After all, there would be a good paycheck for him as well. Following numerous meetings and phone calls, he called one day to say that it might be possible for all parties involved, including the families of the other three women, to settle our suit through mediation, evading a trial by jury. The one critical feature in this was that all four parties had to agree to a solution reached by and with the mediator. The hearing was set for Monday, November 14, 2016, two years and one month following the accident. I reserved a hotel room in Harrisburg, Pennsylvania, where the mediation was to take place. I drove there the previous day, and in a cold, austere hotel room, had a hard time sleeping, wondering about a myriad of things, not the least, what kind of experience this would be. I had never done anything dealing with lawyers and money-related issues previously other than buying and selling a house.

The following morning, we all met in a lawyer's large suite of offices. All the lawyers representing the four women were present. The woman who was in the front seat with Katherine, Jane Zorn, was present and me. No other family members were. The mediator explained the process. He would interview all the lawyers and family members separately, and taking into consideration all the materials he had read about the accident, he would recommend a settlement. This would have to be agreed on by all parties, the trucking company and its insurance company. He said he hoped it could be accomplished that day, but if not, we would have to think about a jury trial.

It was a long day, physically and emotionally exhausting. We were served a tasty lunch and had access to snacks and drinks at any time. The mediator spent, what I figured, an appropriate amount of time with me and asked all the right questions for as much as I could assess. He was very relational, and we engaged in some conversation about religion when he noted that I had a doctorate in ministry from Princeton Seminary. He was a Presbyterian elder, and so we shared some small talk about the present state of the church.

As late afternoon approached, I felt like the day was never going to end. Most of the time, I did some reading and watching cars crossing over the Susquehanna River on Rt. 78 and thought about the many times we crossed that bridge on our various trips. Finally, my lawyer came and revealed they were ready to give the mediator's decision. We all gathered in the big conference room. Obviously, the mediator had met with all the lawyers. Our lawyer indicated there had been some hesitation by a couple of them, but they finally reached an agreement. The mediator informed us of this and then gave instructions about how the lawyers were to proceed. The settlement was not as large as I had anticipated, but it was adequate according to the lawyer.

During the day, I had the opportunity to converse with Jane Zorn. She talked freely about the accident, how she had blacked out and how only later in the hospital became aware that you and Jean were killed. She said it took a couple months for her broken ribs to heal and for her to resume a somewhat normal life following all the trauma she suffered. Since the accident, she had nightmares and was still experiencing them. She was satisfied with the mediation; however, she had received less. Katherine, who was your driver that day, was not present.

It was good to have the whole ordeal finished. Driving home, I felt a certain sense of peace but a sorely aching heart. I was moved to tears repeatedly as I watched trucks speed past, realizing how devastating that accident scene must have been. I have a picture of it on my computer taken from the newspaper. I can't believe you were seated in the back seat of that demolished car. I wonder how you were even removed from the vehicle!

Our lawyer assured me that he would take care of everything. In an appropriate amount of time, all the checks were sent. I forwarded the checks for Karen and Richelle and set up an account in my name as trustee for the care of Candice, with Karen to be trustee, when I am no longer able. For all of us, it was bittersweet money, but it has enabled me to do a couple of things I probably would not have done. It has also precipitated rethinking my will. I wish you were available to make some of those decisions. I already have given and loaned some money to our oldest grandsons to help with their education, very sure this would meet your approval!

Miss you so much working through all this!

Hugs and kisses!

Eating and Living Here

We shared much cooking in our last years together.

Hello, darling.

Today I want to share some thoughts about eating and cleaning up without you. I hate it; that is, I hate eating alone, but then I don't always want to eat with others either. Most men, and some women, wonder and often ask how I am cooking and eating. Some women feel sorry for me and ask if I need any help. Numerous men say they would not know how to go about preparing meals so they would eat out most of the time. That would be more distasteful than eating at home alone—in a restaurant with all kinds of people eating with family and friends, engaging in conversations, and there I am with a plate of food, and that is it. Not for me! I have made dates with a few women for dinner occasionally, primarily because I feel like a nice meal in a restaurant with a female companion, and some interesting

36

conversation is good for me. However, most of the time I eat at home and eat well, maybe too well. In fact, at present, I am dieting with the hope of losing the weight I have gained.

As you know, my cooking goes back to the arrangement we made when you were selling real estate, maybe even before when you were working at Fellowship Bookstore. Because of the evening schedule, I had to eat at a certain time to fit in meetings and counseling. We arrived at a solution by sharing meal preparation, worked for both of us! Additionally, it gave opportunity to work at cooking as a hobby, and I still see it that way most of the time. I enjoyed cooking during college and seminary years, although I didn't do that much. My mother enjoyed cooking and was a good model. Today, all that pays off. Most nights, I enjoy something that is nutritious and delicious. I read a few cookbooks and magazines to get ideas and also watch on YouTube. I expand or subtract on what I read and then cook with a bit of creativity. You would always compliment my cooking skills. Sometimes I wondered if it was because you truly enjoyed it, or you enjoyed not having to cook on some nights so you could be at your computer, either writing or doing something with the photographs you took that day.

Big problem now is that I'm getting too heavy. Going through the evening meal prep, I usually have a martini or a glass of wine; and of course, that does not reduce the calorie total. Lately I have been trying to cut back. It isn't easy. When there is no one with whom to share a conversation, it is easy to snack and mix a drink. You were so very disciplined with snacks, drinks, and most times, with desserts even though you loved them. I think of that little dish you had for your daily bit of ice cream. You packed it to the brim, no more no less, and no seconds except on a special occasion. I miss that example of self-discipline and can't find those little dishes. What is most missed is the awareness that you were ever looking out for me, how I ate and drank, never letting me overindulge. I need that now!

Food shopping is also difficult. Since food shopping was mostly my task, I don't mind doing it and doing it alone. I liked to take loads of time in the supermarket, and you were always anxious to get what we needed and get out. I don't feel that pressure any longer. Roaming the store, looking at different foods promotes the temptation to buy more than needed, particularly for one person, especially true now since there is a new Wegmans rather near, and I shop there quite often. It is a lot larger and more diverse in its offering than the one we shopped at occasionally in Pennsylvania. Because I often buy more than needed, I feel guilty seeing it in the fridge and won't let it go to waste. So here I am about ten pounds heavier than when you left and ever afraid to step on the scale for fear it may be more.

Naturally, you are especially missed at cleanup time. You tended to demand that job for yourself because you were not particularly pleased with my feeble attempts. I recall times when you accused me of doing a bad job on purpose so you would do it. Maybe you were right, but you would be proud of me now. I make sure it is cleaned as you would wish. I hear your voice out there somewhere directing the cleaning of the sink. "Make sure you get off all the scum. Don't leave any residue on the counter!" I even get out the dust broom and sweep the crumbs and whatever most nights.

Talking about cleaning, I am sure you would be curious on how I am maintaining the rest of the place. It was apparent that would be a challenge from my first day alone. Through some of your friends, I found a cleaning lady in Stroudsburg who came out every three weeks. Since I couldn't change the bed with my bad shoulder, neighbors Zorena or Linda helped every week. Some weeks, the cleaning lady would do it. I would often say to myself, after the cleaning lady left and noticed how clean it was, why did Mae always balk at hiring someone to clean? She wasted so much time and effort doing so, and we could afford the cost. But I know there was nothing about cleaning that would meet your approval and goals for perfection. Now in the Jersey condo, I have a cleaning service every other week, and they also change my bed. Since I shower regularly and you or no one else is in bed with me, it works just fine. Two young ladies work for about two hours and even clean the inside of the fridge. I gave away the big vacuum because it is not needed. I use the handheld at times just to pick up stuff swept up from the floor. I think you would be proud of how everything looks, but then again, I don't know for sure.

Just writing about cleaning and food creates the awareness of how well suited we were for each other. Although we had a number of spats, now and then, about food preparation, eating, and cleaning up, we truly enjoyed our togetherness in this area. I am so grateful for how we meshed!

Love you, hon!

A Tough Day

Hi, hon.

I have to share this with you. It has been a tough day. It began with a retired chaplain's visit to June in East Stroudsburg. You remember where she lives, down an unpaved path off Turkey Ridge Drive. Visiting with her touched off feelings of depression. She is a brave lady, and her situation seems to be quite difficult. She is in this remote place, constantly experiencing pain in a knee she doesn't dare get fixed because she would be marooned. She has to depend on different people to provide transportation since she doesn't drive. She also lives very frugally because she doesn't have the resources to do otherwise. She still does all the work around the house and yard, and I am sure you remember that the yard was quite large. We went to the Asian Buffet for lunch, which she enjoys. She said she only gets about two hot meals a week because she no longer cares to cook. She does have future opportunities to escape that setting. Nieces and nephews in New York State promise her care when she is ready. Recently she put her house up for sale.

Anyway, from there, I went to visit Tom and Mary who now own our home. First, I rode around September Circle and noticed how nice all the houses and yards looked and remembered our morning walks along the circle. I recalled some remarks you would make about the houses, how you liked the one those two men, Virgil and Howie, owned, and also the one next door that was built high up. All those thoughts came bumping around my mind and brought tears. Then I drove on to Sunrise Drive to our house. Don was in his yard across the street, and I paused as I rode by and told him I would stop on my way out. His house looked more attractive than ever. It had been painted and a large deck was added on the west end.

When I got to our house, Tom and Mary were happy to see me and invited me in to see "my house." They call it Andy and Mae's house because that is what all the neighbors call it. They have kept it up as you would approve. We sat on the deck they had recently painted with a sealer kind of paint, made especially for decks. Mary served iced tea, and I sat and looked at the trees which have grown taller and provided that wonderful shade from the afternoon sun. The whole experience got to me. What a nice house we had! It looked better than ever, and I realized how I miss it and the whole neighborhood.

After spending some time in the front yard looking at the bushes Mary had recently planted, I left and stopped to talk with Dave and Zorena next door. It was good seeing them again, and we exchanged news about our kids. Xavier has graduated from Temple, and Vanesa is in the army and has a baby. So they were proud to announce they are grandparents. Again, I invited them to stop and see my place since they often travel to New York on Highway 80.

Next, I went across the street to Don and Linda's place. It looks gorgeous. It has become all they intended it to be and all accomplished through their efforts. Don built this deck on the west side of the house that is massive, and with the best wood and steel. The view is incredible. You remember how you could look all the way down and as far out over the trees as our eyes would allow? Now nothing is obstructing that view, and a crowd of people can gather there and enjoy the view and one another's friendship. It is simply delightful. I took a couple pictures.

The ride home was somber. I put on some music, took my time on a not-overly-busy Highway 80. When I got home, I simply made a salad for dinner. I had eaten sufficient at the buffet. It was an evening when I missed you more than ever. The feelings of grief seemed to be ever present. They simply pop up at the most unexpected times, set off by the strangest incidents.

Miss you so much.

Cheated

⟨❧⟩

Dear Mae,

Recently, I went to visit Frank. You remember him from the Chevron Gas Station down the street in Pompton Plains. His story is very sad. While I was in Florida in March, they had a twenty-four-inch snowfall in Pompton Plains. You would have loved it, the kind of snow fall you always desired so you could take pictures of all the beautiful scenes. I remember days after snow falls like that when we would go with our shovels and help some of the older people in our congregation clean their sidewalks and driveways. We loved it, treated it as a winter adventure.

Anyway, after that big snowfall, Frank and his wife Ann went out to do snow removal from their home on the Boulevard, she with her shovel and Frank using his truck with a plow. In the process of cleanup, she got behind the truck. She evidently didn't hear him, had left her hearing aids in the house, and he didn't see her. The result was he backed into her, knocked her over, and she hit her head on the pavement. A few hours later, she died at Chilton hospital from the head injuries.

As you can imagine, he was devastated; and in the course of conversations with Pastor Kathleen, he asked if I would get in touch with him. I did shortly after returning from Florida. I spent a couple hours with him the first time and also at other times as well. He especially wanted me to share how I survived your sudden loss. I am going to continue visiting with him. Next time, I will invite him to see the condo here in Wharton. I want to help him visualize a way to get beyond his present state. He seemed overwhelmed at the moment, and I wanted to show him that for all of us, there is a possible new future. He is not ready for that now. Hopefully I can plant seeds that build hope.

Anyway, back to the real purpose I am writing this letter. Frank talked often yesterday about how he feels cheated. He and Ann were both sixty-seven. He had just sold the station. Their son Frank lives in Florida, and they were hoping to begin to do some traveling, even thinking about a river cruise in Europe. He also owns a nice condo in Florida on Hutchinson Island. It reminded me that this is also how I feel so much of the time—cheated. We had been quite busy since retirement. I had done a couple interims and then was hit with non-Hodgkin's lymphoma, stem-cell transplant, shoulder surgery, and prostate cancer. You were at the point where you were confident about how to handle your bowel problems. We were both ready to begin a new, less active, more relaxed phase of life, perhaps even find a condo some place and sell the house, at least do some interesting travel.

Just before you were killed, we had talked with Wes and Phyl about a river cruise through some of the reformation spots in Europe the following year, and Phyl was going to check it out. You had also questioned me about moving back to New Jersey. You said, "You promised that we would live here for ten years and then begin to think of moving back closer to the girls. It's been ten years now." I think of that often, especially as I enjoy and see other couples participate in all the opportunities of living in this condo complex. I say to myself, "Mae would enjoy this immensely, and there would be so much we could be enjoying together with other couples." Being alone just isn't what it would have been here with you.

Frank feels cheated, and well, he should, and so do I. I feel cheated of the good healthy years we could have done things together, time on the golf course, even times with you at the shore, although you know that wasn't among my favorite places. Nonetheless, I always enjoyed those short stays we had there. Although I didn't appreciate the hot sand, I did enjoy the ocean sounds and breezes and your adventuresome desire to jump in the waves. You were always so alive at the shore, so full of fun bristling over with ideas. Our rides home with ice cream cones were never boring.

Despite the heavy traffic, we always enjoyed each other's company and conversation. Many new ideas were born in those discussions. We talked often on those rides about how our lives would come to an end some day and our wonderful relationship would be broken. We were both so certain that I would leave first and how each might have to manage without the other. I think you may have prepared your mind for it more than me. After all, you had all that time to think about it during the period of my cancer treatments and stem cell transplant. You saw me almost die that night after the replacement and kept yourself together marvelously. You were always a person of great faith. One of the reasons I loved you so much. Losing you at any time, I would have felt cheated; but losing you when I did, when we were so ready to live more fully, really hurts. I was cheated!

Let me end this telling you about last night. I felt cold in bed. It was hot outside, but I like it cold when I sleep. And you did too so we could snuggle. I set the AC on 68 and in the middle of the night, got up and added a blanket that I had removed after the cleaning women made the bed. I must have fallen right to sleep because I dreamt you said to me, "Why did you add that blanket? I was warm enough." You were more than warm, honey. You were hot! I was cheated when I lost you.

Love, hugs, and kisses.

"Our days at the shore were always great because
you loved the water so much"

Friends

Hi, hon.

Just wanted to talk with you tonight about some of our friends. This afternoon, I went to the viewing of Lillian Grimbilas, Ken's mother. She lived to be ninety-four, a very active and charitable life. Tomorrow they will have a mass at Our Lady of Good Counsel. I will go. She was a woman who had to deal with much disappointment in her life, even though they were financially successful. She is an example of the truth that it is not what you possess but the faith that pervades your life. You remember her daughter Marilyn; I performed the wedding for her and Bruce at the church some years ago. Ken built a ramp so she could be brought down the aisle and reach the altar area despite her disability.

It made me aware again of how important our friends have been through our lives every place we lived. Ken and Nancy were among the good friends we had in Pompton Plains. There were so many good friends everywhere we lived. Sometimes I wonder if we were as supportive and helpful to them as they were to us. Now that you are gone, I realize more than ever how important friends are. I was also reminded of this today after inviting Frank up for lunch. I think his loss of Ann hurts more than my losing you, at least at this time, not that you were less important to me than Ann was to him but because the manner in which she died, and he feels responsible.

Again, I was struck by how much his friends mean for him. They often stay with him overnight because they fear that depression might takeover and become so severe that he might be susceptible to suicide. I don't think so because he shows a lot of growth emotionally in his first two months after loss. He has a very extensive connection of friends on so many levels. He has them because he was always ready to help people. I remember how he went out of his way to help us dispose of Candice's last car. I think you always had a more connected set of friends than I did. You worked at making friends, and I don't think I did like you. So many people wanted to be my friend because I held a rather prominent position, and often I kind of kept at a distance because I wanted time by myself and felt so much of my life was helping people, sometimes people that really irritated me. I hate to say that, but as you know, it was true. You always cautioned me on this because you were aware, but now I realize more than ever how important friends are. And I have to be more grateful for all the friends that became part of our life.

One of the blessings of living in this new condo complex is that I have to make new friends. I really miss you in that process! When we moved to Pennsylvania, we had a lot of almost instant friends, some of them due to our worshipping at Shawnee Presbyterian Church and joining Shawnee Country Club and because of your involvement in Red Hats and the adult education opportunities at East Stroudsburg University Adult Learning Center. I'm just not a joiner like you. My father would often comment about me saying, "I don't know how I raised such an independent kid." And that was not a compliment but rather a statement about my unwillingness to get involved with others at times when he thought I should. One of the prime reasons you meant so much to me was your gregarious personality. You made up for what was lacking in me and enabled us to be a couple that could build and appreciate the community.

It's getting late, and I am tired. I will write again soon. I was hoping this writing would help me deal with the emptiness I feel, and I guess it does, but tonight I especially feel your loss. It comes and goes, and tonight it has come bigly, as President Trump would say. I still need to write to you about him. He was elected two years after your death. So I wish you could have experienced him. I would love to hear your judgement! I doubt very much you would have cared for him.

Enough for tonight. Love you as much as ever!

Daughter Richelle's Visit

Good morning, hon. Yesterday Richelle arrived to be with me for a week. It was so good to see her. She has been very disciplined and has lost weight. She is in good shape, walks regularly just like Karen. I found it difficult getting around the airport. I am experiencing increasing difficulty with balance. One of the things I no longer dare do is go down an escalator. Going up is okay, but going down makes me feel like I am going to fall. It always reminds of that time in Tokyo when we had to lug all our baggage down the escalator at the airport. Already at that time, I was uneasy getting on, and that was one of the longest and highest I ever experienced.

Richelle's bag came quickly. And although we had a long walk to where I could park, we made it easily, and the ride home brought us past Wegmans where we stopped to get some groceries. They built a new Wegmans in Parsippany. You would love it. It has everything, especially a nice seafood section. We bought some scallops and salmon which we will eat while she is here. Last night, we went to eat at the neighborhood Italian place just off the gate of our complex. Food is good, but they are in the process of renovation, and the menu is limited. We had fried calamari and shrimp parmesan.

Richelle was supposed to go with Karen to do painting at an event that Karen had arranged. They did that last year when Richelle was here. This year, she was too tired, and I didn't feel like running her to Ridgewood where they were to meet. Having been awakened early California time to get here and in the process losing three hours, she was so tired she fell asleep on the couch and went to bed early.

She was able to do a number of things here that she truly enjoyed. She went to the shore with Karen, Bruce, and all the kids, plus a young girl, Karlee's age, from France who is staying with them for a few days. She is the daughter of one of the friends Karen made when she worked for that French perfume company. Richelle said that the water was cold. I wonder if it would have been too cold for you to jump around in the waves as you always did. I met them back at Karen's and ate there after they arrived home.

The peak experience for her week was being able to go with Karen on Sunday to see the musical *Hamilton* in New York. I asked her what she wanted to do while here; and she responded, saying she wanted to go into the city, perhaps see the 9/11 Memorial. I said I would go in with her, but because it was predicted to be very hot, I reneged. I just didn't want to risk all that traffic on either train, bus, or car with my limited flexibility and increasing lack of balance. I suggested she might like to see a play with Karen. I would gift them both tickets and suggested she check out *Hamilton*. When she began to look at ticket prices, she found them abysmally costly. Finally, using StubHub, she found two for about 500 dollars apiece; and I gladly put them on my American Express. I just had the feeling you would approve and really saw their attendance as a way to remember you for all the encouragement you gave in their love for drama.

On Sunday, when they went in, it was very hot, and they had to stand in line outside the theatre for about twenty minutes. Karen wasn't feeling well, but once they got in, they enjoyed it tremendously. Karen drove in with her little Mini Cooper, and then they drove back here to the condo where I had made corn beef and cabbage in a slow cooker. Karlee stayed with me because Bruce and Garrett had gone to their place in Pennsylvania. Richelle and I did visit Candice on Saturday. That visit was not good at all, and I am not going to comment on it right now. I will wait for another time after I have dealt with some of my own issues and can talk about it more objectively. Let me just say now that Candice is very sick, and I have to discover more about her condition prior to writing about it.

The last day Richelle was here, she wanted to go to Clifton just to see our old neighborhood, and I suggested we have lunch at Matthew's, which used to be Bella Napoli where we have had a good number of family celebrations. We had a wonderful lunch. Richelle had one of the waitresses take our picture, and she shared it on Facebook. The food in the restaurant is as good as ever, maybe better; and the configuration is the same, only with improvement of ambiance. After lunch, we went to Applegate in Montclair and had ice cream and then went past the church, which is now a mosque, parsonage, friends' homes, and your parents' home. Richelle just wanted to bask in the memory of it all. We concluded our trip down memory lane with a ride through downtown Montclair and a look at what used to be Fellowship Bookstore.

We had planned to spend the last evening with Bruce and Karen and family here, ordering in pizza. They all came, except for Karen who wasn't feeling well. She has had a lot of trouble with her stomach lately, and they don't seem to be able to find the cause or enable a cure. I am a bit concerned for a number of reasons but will also save that for another letter. We all had enough pizza, and they stayed around for a couple hours as we watched the Mets game. The ride to the airport the following morning went well, and she had a fine trip back to Los Angeles, where Gerry met her at the airport. I wish you could have been with us. Richelle's presence made me even more grateful for the kind of mother you were. Richelle radiates the love and care you had for your family and all others. She is so helpful and easy to be with, so like you! She is also getting to resemble you more as she grows older. She seems to be well at ease with her place in life and faces all her challenges with a sense of well-being and hope that things will work out.

Bye for now. I will write more later in the week. I am presently preparing to preach at Pompton Plains on Sunday. I am a bit anxious because I know the energy it demands, and I don't possess what I used to have.

Love ya, hon!

"Richelle's visits are always a pleasure. Her demeanor
is so much like yours, so helpful and kind"

My Last Sermon

Hi, hon. I preached on Sunday, July 8, and it went very well. It did exhaust me. Fortunately, when I got home, I went to the pool and just floated around a while and then spent some time in the hot tub. It helped me feel partially refreshed.

I preached on a text from Mark, the seventh chapter verses 24 through 37. Mark tells about a break Jesus took; he left Galilee to go to Tyre where he met the Syrophoenician woman, and then he went back to Galilee where on the way, he ran into a deaf and dumb man. I shared the idea that each of these encounters were serendipitous and because he was away on break, he didn't necessarily want to be engaged. In the first encounter with the woman, she asked him to cast out the evil spirit in her daughter. He responded by saying that the children need to be first fed the bread from the table, and only after that do the dogs get food. I'm sure you remember that story.

Using those stories as the subject matter, I asked the question, "do you make a difference with your life?" pointing to Jesus as the one who, in these instances, made a difference. I highlighted three things about the action of Jesus. One, he learned the need for openness. In making that very striking statement about the bread for the children and crumbs for the dogs, he was giving evidence of his prejudice, of the fact that having grown up in the Jewish culture, he saw his first responsibility to *only* the Jews. When the woman responded to his ironic statement with, "Yes, but even the dogs get the crumbs from the children's table," he had a wow moment. He realized that this foreign woman, this Greek woman, was also a woman of faith; and he responded to her with his healing presence. In those moments, Jesus learned of his own prejudice, and he needed to change. To make a difference, he had to become aware, had to learn that not only were the Jews to be treated with his healing blessing, but he had come for all people. To make a difference, we also needed to learn and become cognizant of the fact that people that are different from us can also be people of faith who need to be loved and cared for even as we care for our own tribe.

My second thought was that Jesus was present to the moment. Even on break, he was able to respond to a need because he was present to what was happening *now*. We are so often so into ourselves and what we want that we miss being aware of needs all around us. He was aware, and because of that awareness, he was a blessing.

The last thought was that Jesus was faithful to his calling, his purpose for being. I referred to his speech in the synagogue (Luke 4) in his hometown where he quoted Isaiah about being anointed to bring good news to the poor. I emphasized that he did not work for success but to be faithful to his calling. That is how he made the difference with his life and how we can do the same.

So I wish you could have heard it and given me the feedback you always did so graciously. You never came at me with a negative argument about my thoughts but always enabled me to look at what I said in a broader context. You had a unique way of helping me see that there might be a better way of saying something, at the same time affirming me. I really miss that kind of mutual affirming relationship. Now that I no longer preach, I will be listening to sermons thinking about how you might respond to them, always knowing that you would first find something good in each of them.

I really figure this will be the last time I preach. It has been a tough decision, but I feel it—tougher because I received an ovation following the sermon, and it is tough giving up that type of affirmation for something you know you do well and have for many years. One reason for quitting is lacking in energy and stamina. I have accepted a request to preach in Pompton Lakes in a couple of weeks but may cancel because I'm having some severe sciatic pain at present and think that it is somewhat stress-related to taking on too much visiting and speaking. I'm also feeling that my body is beginning to suffer from all the chemo bombardment, stem-cell replacement, MRIs, and CAT scans I endured when fighting the non-Hodgkin's cancer, not to mention the shoulder surgery following and then radiation for prostate cancer. I remember with so much gratitude how you struggled through it all with me. In those thirty days at Hackensack Hospital in isolation for the stem cell replacement, you only missed one day, and that was so you could get the house cleaned properly for my return home. Dirt and dust were prohibited following the stem cell, and you were going to make sure that rule was followed. You always showed so much love and compassion. You let your tears flow easily, and we had so many of them together during the time of recovery. Honey, I will never forget. You were so good.

I need to add some more before I conclude this letter. I have definitely decided to stop preaching. I did preach at Pompton Lakes, not on the first date they asked me but a few Sundays later. Like Pompton Plains, they livestream their worship. Only they preserve the video for what it seems is eight to ten weeks. At Pompton Plains, it is only live, although they do have an audio podcast library they preserve. This enabled me to view the service on Monday morning, not pleasant! I noted just how much slower I am in moving about, in figuring out the flow of the service (Worldwide Communion) in reading, stumbling over a number of words, and failing to put emphasis where needed because of diminished vision. I did okay, and people were complimentary. But what I witnessed confirmed the reality that enough is enough. I had a great run in the pulpit. It all began with the preaching prize for the best preacher in seminary, and I have had opportunities to preach in some outstanding pulpits, including Princeton University Chapel. Now I know it is over. I still have to respond to a couple of tentative requests for the Advent Season and say "thanks, but no thanks." It is kind of sad, but I am good with it.

Maybe if you were still here, I might continue. I need your help now just to get ready, tie buttons to get dressed, help me figure out what to wear, all stuff about which I was completely independent— not any more, hon! I feel more dependent than ever.

Love ya, babe. More soon!

Your Friend Is Dying

Good day, honey.

It is kind of a tough day. I got a late start, slept too long. I woke up in the middle of the night with chest pains. I am sure it was gas because it moved around, and after I got up to use the bathroom and drank some water, I was finally able to get to sleep and had a hard time waking at 8:30 a.m. However, the chest pains did provoke some anxiety because earlier in the evening, I talked with Don Postema who suffered a heart attack last week. When he described his symptoms, he mentioned chest pains that would not go away. I probably remembered some of that conversation as I experienced those pains in the middle of the night.

Also I had a rather difficult day yesterday. Your friend Roseann is dying of brain cancer. Yesterday, Pete and her sister Donna staged a birthday party for her at the Shawnee Fire Department building to which a large crowd of people were invited. Many were from the Presbyterian Church we attended in Shawnee. Pete particularly invited me to be present and asked me to be responsible for the memorial service when that time comes. There were a good number of our friends present, members from Shawnee Presbyterian Church, red hats, and Shawnee Golf Club people. Roseann was there on a gurney with a hospice nurse at her side. Karl and Dale were there, and Pete wanted Karl and me to say a prayer. I left home with a variety of feelings related to the fact that Pete asked me to do the memorial service. After all, Karl was their pastor for so many years, as well as a good friend. Just subsequently, Pete informed me that Karl is not allowed to do anything pastoral at Shawnee because of Presbyterian rules for retired ministers—in my mind, a stupid rule. Karl was close to both of them and should have been able to do that memorial since the church doesn't have a pastor at this time. I also understand he will do a graveside service at the burial site in Roseann's hometown. He is allowed because it is not in Shawnee. Some rules I don't approve!

Today is dreary as well. We are going to have rain for the next five or six days, and Karen and family are at Virginia Beach for their vacation week. It's not going to be very nice for them if they are thinking of going into the water and being on the beach. I tried to call Karen last night but couldn't get her, so I will try again today. I definitely need to do some exercise to get me out of this funk I'm experiencing. I have also had some problems with the sciatic nerve, and it seems to affect my entire outlook. Funny how a simple pain in the back and leg can have such an effect on one's attitude. I guess it really is a combination of a number of things.

Tomorrow, I will make a retiree-chaplain visit to Frank Villerius and his friend Mary. Reaching out always seems to generate a more positive attitude. I have found that when I am alone and inactive, there is a tendency to play the "pity pot" game. Everything begins to hurt. I don't want to talk with anyone; and I need to push myself to get up, get out, and do something that helps someone else. Some of the women friends whom I have made and have also lost their mates seem to be better able to do this than me. It seems that women are more natural nurturers, which I think happens because of their bringing children into the world and caring for them so much of the time during their younger years while we men were out doing what we thought were the more important things. Too bad we fooled ourselves so badly! I think that is evolving quite a bit with this younger generation.

Love ya, hon, and miss you so much!

In a Funk

Hi, hon.

I'm feeling very needy and sad! I feel just miserable! I felt there was no reason to get out of bed this morning. You have been gone almost four years now, and one would think that I should be pretty well adjusted to being alone. I am not. I hate it! I was always so accustomed to have you near. I took it for granted and am really feeling it now.

This morning I went to the "Option B" friends page on Facebook to read about people grieving. I listened to the speech Sheryl Sandberg gave at a university graduation. I have heard it before but really needed to hear it again. She challenged me to realize how necessary it is to put aside "pity pot" feelings and begin to find new ways to reach out helping others find hope and meaning. I feel selfish this morning and want people to do that for me. I know there are people just waiting to do that, especially some women, but chose not to make myself vulnerable. I have an invitation for lunch and a boat ride following with two widows tomorrow. I will go but don't want to, would rather be by myself here at the condo and know that is the worst thing I could do. I will go feeling bad inside and all the time pretending all is right in my world as I do so often. I figure people expect that of me given my station in life as a pastor. All the time, I will feel dishonest with them and myself.

I have made a friend who was also a pastor. When he retired, he chose to shed his title. He wants no one to know, and in sharing, he requested I not reveal it. He told me because he knew my history of theological education in the Reformed community, and we knew some of the same persons along our journey. This week we enjoyed a glass of wine together, and as we talked, I had to reflect that maybe if I had not been so open about being clergy, I would be freer to be more vulnerable. But then I realized going back to worship at Pompton Plains and preaching at various churches in the area keeps me from being unknown. He can do so because he has divorced himself from where he was pastor and most of the people in that part of his life. It wouldn't be a solution for me, I know.

Perhaps some of this feeling of despair is related to pain I am experiencing from a sciatic condition. It began about two weeks ago and seems to be aggravated by walking. I feel it is so important to walk. It is not only an enjoyable exercise but enables the mind to reflect in positive ways about almost everything. Idleness promotes depression. I need to be about and doing, which also generates good feelings. If I don't keep moving, it cuts back on metabolism, and this only adds to weight gain. And I want to lose weight, not gain.

As I write, Pete called. Roseann died this morning. A couple weeks ago, I promised him and her sister Donna that I would do a memorial service. I can feel the adrenaline of being notified. An obligation to which I am committed and sharing with Pete during this time of initial grieving gets me going and dampens the depression. Even the nerve pain seems less. I will meet for lunch with Pete on Tuesday and make plans for the memorial. The funeral will be a simple graveside in Mechanicsburg, Pennsylvania, where she was born and raised. Karl Viernstein will do that. It will take place next week and the memorial service in Shawnee at a time convenient to Pete and myself. We have settled on August 28. Taking on a commitment like this is difficult, and I wonder why I say yes to these requests. Perhaps it is my ego getting in the way, I have to work on this! Why can't I just enjoy being not always having to do something significant? I can help someone just by being a friend. There are others who can do memorial services. Sorry I had to unload all this, but it is perhaps good!

Well, I led the memorial service. It was on Tuesday of this week and at 11:00 a.m. in Shawnee Presbyterian Church, probably the largest crowd in that church for decades. Pete said it was the largest crowd he had ever seen there. He and Roseann's sister spoke, also her best friend whose name escapes me. Midge and Dale both sang. Beautiful! Again, Karl was not there because of the Presbyterian's rule about retired pastors and their former church.

My part consisted of Scripture reading, the eulogy, and a brief homily. I put together my memories of Roseann with some shared by friends and family members. The brief homily was on the story of Jesus raising Lazarus. It all went very well. A number of people said it was the most meaningful funeral they had ever attended. I guess statements like that only prove we all have short memories. You would have appreciated being there and meeting your many friends who have befriended me since your loss. Love ya.

Candice

Dearest Mae,

In one of the previous letters, I mentioned a visit with Candice while Richelle was here. It turned out to be a very difficult visit, and ever since, I have been bothered. At this time in her journey, she does not believe I am her father, that I am someone else with a Dutch name she uses, and I can't understand. She brought that up again when Richelle and I visited. I showed her a family picture with all of us, and she responded by saying she was just posing. She was not in the picture as a family member. Richelle immediately said, "Candice, you are my sister. You are part of our family." Candice became very irritated and began yelling at us, saying she was not part of our family. We tried nicely to tell her she was, and she became increasingly agitated. She wanted us to leave and got up and yelled at us to get out. The social worker on duty said, "Candice, that is not a nice way to talk to your family." Her response was to tell him to shut up, it was none of his business.

We left, of course, in tears. We realized that staying on would upset the whole house. There were a couple of the other women there, and we didn't want to frighten them. We didn't try to connect with her afterward either. Karen gave her a small iPad on which we can Skype her since she does not have a phone. We try to do that now and then, but haven't recently. Last night, I tried, and she answered, "Hello?" But when she discovered it was me, she hung up. This is very troubling. I am always wondering if she would do that with you. I can't help thinking that some of her confusion has to be related to the grief experience of your loss which she never acknowledges or even mentions.

Earlier this week, I had lunch with Bob Parker (CEO of Newbridge Services which maintains the home and service Candice has). I called him and asked to just check how she was doing because we can't find out any information due to the HIPAA mandate. When we met, he did tell me that she is safe, and the administrator of the program says not to worry about her. I guess I will just have to adjust to having her out of my life. In a sense, she has been dead to us for years because her schizophrenia has destroyed the person she was before her illness. But she is still alive, and I love her. The desire to connect with her will never vanish.

I asked Parker for some suggestions on how I can deal with this, and he suggested finding a group of family members. He is going to check on some existing groups and get back to me. You used groups when she first became ill and know that it was very helpful. I avoided them. I don't know why. I think it was because I was so involved in group dynamics with my work I didn't want to get in another group. Now I no longer have all those contacts and may need to find a group. Another reason is being a pastor, I always see myself as a healer, even in a group. I find it hard to admit to myself that I am the one needing the healing.

It is also true that you were my healer. You always knew the right thing to say to Candice. You knew how to listen to her in a way that enabled her to keep connected with us. Ever since you left, we all have had a problem relating to her. It began immediately with the challenge of handling her money. She didn't really want me to take over, and eventually the Newbridge administration has taken over. There doesn't seem to be any problem with that. She seems to have what she wants and needs. In fact, she had enough to give us all gift cards for Christmas. It will be interesting to see what happens this Christmas. She doesn't acknowledge any of our birthdays.

You are sorely missed as my guide and counselor!

Love ya.

Lost Billfold

———— ✑ ————

Dear Mae,

You will never know how much you were missed last night. It had been a good day. I did some reading and writing in the morning and then went for rehab at the medical pavilion in the early afternoon. Arriving at home, I emptied my pockets, put the key in the basket on the table, got a piece of fruit out of the fridge, and proceeded to do some more writing. The afternoon passed quickly, and just like that, it was time to start making dinner. I had a delicious meal of sautéed scallops and mixed vegetables, a recipe I created. After cleanup, I watched a ball game.

When bedtime arrived, I proceeded to undress, plug in my phone, and pick up my billfold and place it in the tray where I keep it each night. Trouble was I couldn't find the billfold. I had no idea where I put it. I looked and looked and looked some more but no billfold. I even went down to the car twice to see if I left it there—no luck, no billfold! What was I going to do? If only Mae was here, she would know the next move and probably have the eyes to find it! Oh Mae, where are you? I need you so much. You would find that billfold. Panic was beginning to set in. What should I do first? At such a time, I don't seem to be able to hold it together anymore. It's eleven forty-five now, too late to call anyone. I'm convinced I'm not going to get any sleep all night, better at least call American Express and Citi Bank about the missing credit cards (thankfully only carry those two).

Then there is also my military ID, the new Medicare card, New Jersey driver's license, and other membership cards. Should I get in the car and drive down to where I parked for rehab? Can't, don't have my license! Maybe I better call the credit card companies first, or maybe the police, report the loss. What is the police number? I went to my cell phone, now almost out of battery, plugged it into the charger, and asked Siri for the Rockaway Police number. She gives it, and I call. Message must have been confusing to the officer on the other end because he finally said, "You want to report a lost wallet?"

"Yes!"

"And what is your address?" I gave it and then asked if he knew where that was and how he could get into our community.

"Don't worry, I will send out an officer to make a report, and he will know how to get in. We have been there before."

Good, at least now someone will come to talk with me; but in the meantime, I should get busy and cancel those credit cards, or maybe not. Maybe I need to wait until after the police report. I am confused, don't know what to do and no one to ask! I never missed having you there to advise so much as in those moments! I feel horrid. My heart is beating heavy, and I feel a bit short of breath. Oh, how is this going to turn out? I get on the computer and look up the American Express account. I don't have the card on which I would usually get the telephone number. These websites…as I begin to look for a phone number, it is the last thing to be found. Finally I get it, and now the phone rings. It is the police at the front door, and I respond by pressing no. 6 to let him in. Shortly there is a knock on the door, and a very friendly looking police officer has arrived.

He begins by asking a host of questions: When did I last use it? Where was I? What color is it? What does it contain? and a lot of others which I answered. Then he suggests that we look around the condo. Where was I sitting? Together we dig down into each chair used that night, found a few coins but no billfold. We look in every room, including the bathroom, still no billfold. Then he asks if I checked out the car to see if it was left there. "Yes," I said, "went down and looked twice."

"How about where you parked at rehab? Could you have dropped it while getting in the car?

"Perhaps, but I can't go now without a license."

"Well, I can go there and look after we put together a report. Just give me a general idea where you parked. The pavilion is closed now, and if they had found it, they would have undoubtedly called. But first let's both go down to the car."

So I get the key, and we get on the elevator and head down. I open the driver's seat door. He checks the pocket in the door where I usually keep junk. I notice that it definitely needs to be cleaned out. He then gets in the driver's seat, reaches down in the cup holders where there are a couple of pairs of glasses, and pulls up an item—a black billfold. He holds it up, looks at me, and asks, "Is this it?"

Hooray! Hallelujah! Yes! Yes! Yes! "Where was it?" I ask.

"Right here, in with your glasses," he responds.

Can you believe it! In the last half hour, I went to that car twice, sat in the seat, looked at everything I thought, and never saw it because it wasn't where I usually placed it.

Well, I am sure you could imagine how relieved I felt. And all this would undoubtedly not have happened if you were here. On our first trip to the car, you would have spotted it. I will write a thank you to the Rockaway police, and since I got the officer's name, I will give thanks for his service. Feeling it would be hard getting to sleep, I took half of a sleeping medication. Slept well!

Living without your love and presence will never be easy, especially when challenged with these kinds of incidents!

Love ya.

Andrew

Karen

———— ✺ ————

Hi, hon.

This has been a tough couple of weeks. On Friday, two weeks ago, Bruce called to tell me about Karen's condition. She has been having trouble swallowing and experiencing discomfort in her intestinal tract. Up to this point, her doctors have been attributing it to acid reflux. They have put her on various medications with no significant change in her condition. In fact, last weekend, she stayed home most of the time, too weak to get up and do things and unable to eat. She has also been losing weight.

Because of her frustration with lack of improvement, she found a new doctor and had an appointment on Thursday. He was also a GI type, and after examination, he felt it was more than a GI tract problem. It must have to do with her heart, and after discovering that the next appointment she had with her heart doctor was October, he contacted his heart guy and was able to arrange an appointment for the next day. When she met with him, he felt there might be a blockage in the coronary artery. "After all," he said, "it has been forty-one years, and it could need some repair." So an angiogram was scheduled for the following Monday morning.

We have always been concerned about her health since her open-heart surgery at age twelve. However, you always had that sense of assurance she would survive and be okay when she hit a bump in her health journey. I miss that confident presence and would love to just be able to talk with you, especially hear how you would be measuring the situation. Now my concern is magnified because you are not here to share your advice and assessment of what is happening. Late Friday afternoon, Bruce called to inform me that they were going to do a procedure on her. She was too broken up to talk. I did call her later, and although she was quite weepy, she was able to talk and relate some more info on how she felt. At times, she has shortness of breath. She was quite apprehensive of the procedure but also was anxious to have it because the doctor had told her that if there was blockage, he would insert a stent, and that would resolve the issue.

As the weekend progressed, Karen became increasingly concerned. She didn't go out at all and didn't attend church where Kathleen informed the congregation and requested prayers. I had stopped to see Karen on Saturday, and she just sat in a recliner. I also stopped over Sunday afternoon, and she was in bed but got up and sat in the recliner. And she, Bruce, and I talked. After a very short time, she informed Bruce that she didn't feel good and that she wanted a glass of water. When he got it for her, she took a few sips, but it was obvious she was not feeling well at all. Rather abruptly, she said she wanted to go to the hospital. She was supposed to go and check in later in the afternoon, but she was ready to go right then.

She kissed all the kids, and Bruce carried her to his truck and took off. I thought they should have called an ambulance with all the up-to-date equipment for someone having heart trouble, but she wanted Bruce to take her. Just after they left, one of her friends brought dinner for the evening, and I left for home. Bruce kept in touch, informing me what was occurring and when she finally was placed in a room for the night. I told him I would meet him at the hospital in the morning. Gosh, hon, I so wanted you to be with me, and of course, all of us. The calm nature you created for everyone when things like that occurred was missing. We were all very much on edge, and I thought back to those days we were in New York, anticipating her initial surgery in 1977. I'm sure she remembered all that as well and was very scared. I think not feeling well and asking Bruce to take her to the hospital was triggered by fear. The whole time I felt on the verge of tears. Similar fears to what we felt prior to her surgery back in 1977 seemed to be present again. Fortunately, I was able to sleep that night. I talked with Brother John about it and a few other friends as well, and that served to quiet some of the fears.

I arrived at the hospital the next morning about eleven forty-five. Bruce and Karen were downstairs in the room where she was prepared for the procedure. I talked to them on the cell phone and stayed next to the coffee shop where I was told to wait. While ordering a cup of coffee, a fellow in a hospital gown tapped me on the shoulder and said, "Did you play golf at Shawnee?" I said yes and realized it was a fellow named Mark whose last name I forgot. He had been a member at Shawnee Country Club during our time there, and I had played a number of tournaments with him. We exchanged pleasantries and memories for a brief few minutes, and then he said he had to get down where he worked. Turned out, he was one of the PAs that worked in the procedure room where Karen's doctor did his thing. I told him to go say hello to Karen. Once he did that, Bruce and one of his friends, who also worked there, came up and invited me down to the waiting area. Arriving there, I met and talked with the doctor.

It was only a short time until they took Karen. Bruce and I went up to the cafeteria for lunch. Rather soon, we were informed by a buzzer that Karen was ready to come out. When we went down, we had to wait a few minutes; and the doctor came out to inform us that her artery was clear, no need for a stent. Perhaps she would need some medications, but he was not sure. She would need further testing both by him and the GI doctor. It took a while for Karen to awake. When she became aware, she was not too happy about the results. Her anticipation was that with a stent, all the tightness in the throat and stomach acid reflux would disappear.

Since then, she has suffered a rather difficult couple of weeks. First, there was the wrist healing where they inserted the prob; and then her stomach has been upset, not wanting to eat and almost too weak to get out of bed. She seems to be gaining strength and finding an appetite but still is very concerned because the symptoms remain. I think Karen especially misses you at a time like this, and I definitely know I do. I doubt I have been as aware as I need to be about how much all the girls miss you. So much of the time, I am concerned about how much I miss you I forget about them.

As the days passed, Karen continued to have problems. She now has an appointment with an ENT doctor who seems to think her problem is the vagus nerve which controls many of the involuntary actions of body parts such as the heart, lungs, intestinal tract. She will have more tests. My immediate concern is her anxiety. Because one of chief symptoms is the contracting of her throat muscles, it restricts breathing and scares her into feeling she can't breathe. I am sure some of this is related to her basic anxiety about it all. She has also made an appointment with a counselor. Since this whole thing will continue, I will be writing to you more about it I am sure.

Love you and could use some good hugs right now!

McCain's Funeral

Good afternoon, darling!

I spent most of this morning, Sept. 1, 2018, watching the funeral service of John McCain on television. Surprisingly, almost all the major cable stations carried it without commercials and any commentary. It was held at the Washington Cathedral and lasted almost three hours. I watched the whole thing, and it brought an array of feelings: sad and glad. I wished so much that we could have watched it together and were able to share thoughts, especially about the music.

When music began, some of it performed by the choir from the Naval Academy, I recognized the tune but could not name the piece. You were always so helpful with this. You knew every tune and would name it. I would have to listen to a few lines sung before I could pick up the words, familiar, but still not enough to name the piece. One song in particular that got to me was "Danny Boy" sung by an excellent woman soloist. When she began, I recognized the tune as one of the hymns we sang in church as kids. Then I realized it was "Danny Boy" and remembered there was a hymn with lyrics written to the tune, but I didn't know the name of the hymn. I said to myself, "If only Mae were here, she would know and start singing it!"

This brings up a whole other series of thoughts. You and I were in sync on so much of life. We could talk about almost any subject and know where the other was coming from. There was no lack of understanding between us although there could be disagreement. Most of the time, it seemed to me that our disagreements were opportunities to enlarge our views on whatever we were discussing or debating. I guess this wasn't so true in our early years together, but as our experiences ripened, our understanding of each other grew "EST" (the Werner Erhardt series of lectures, now called *The Landmark*, was especially helpful. It got us both realizing we didn't always have to be right, but we needed to be honest and authentic. We began to apply this unintentionally and imperceptibly, and it strengthened our relationship and that with others. It drastically affected the way I went about sermon preparation. Rather than always trying to quote what others said about a text, I began to trust my reading of the text and life experience. The Bible became more than a text. It began to provide a broader view of life).

Back to the funeral! There really wasn't much about the gospel in what the clergy shared. They all took a background seat to family and friends in the political world. I liked what George Bush, the younger, said best. Both he and Obama were asked to speak, both rivals who beat McCain. I appreciated Bush because he said what Obama said, only in fewer words, not as articulate but appropriate in time and content. You always liked the fewer words and were ever insistent that when I spoke, I said what needed to be said in the least and most concise words possible. Your attitude was always that the mind could only be engaged by what the seat could endure. Too long in the pew was too much for the whole person to absorb.

One more feature of the funeral was the speech by his daughter Megan. She had the normal difficult time getting through her tears and the speech, but it was all very touching. There probably will be big push backs on things she said that definitely reflected her and the family's disdain for President Trump without using his name. He was not invited and was obviously missed not sitting in the front row with the Obamas, Bushes, and Clintons. Kind of inappropriate, but then when one remembers what Trump said in a campaign situation about McCain, that he didn't respect people who were prisoners of war, he respected winners, one can understand. That would put a dagger in my heart if I were a child in the McCain family. Their father spent at least five years with maximum torture in a Vietnamese prison camp.

Anyway, it was all very moving, and I so wished you had been there so we could exchange comments. I know you wouldn't have been sitting like me. You would have been moving around doing a dozen things but still listening to it all. There was always too much to do for you to just sit for two hours or more.

Love ya, hon!

A Terrible Day

Hi, hon.

This has been one of the worst days since you left. It is Candice's fifty-eighth birthday. Since she chased Richelle and me out the last time we visited, I had some trepidation about visiting but felt compelled to bring a gift on her birthday. I tried to call her on Skype before leaving, but got no response, so I figured I would just go even though she had told me to never come to see her again.

I bought a special card, looked through a couple card racks before I found one that seemed right, put three fifty-dollar bills in the card, and bought a couple different sacks of milk chocolate to put in a gift bag with the card. I rode through a terrible rainstorm on that road we used to take as a shortcut out of Boonton because I didn't want to be on 80 with all the rain. When I got there, the lady in charge for the day greeted me warmly and said she would see that Candice came down from her room. She knew it was her birthday, and they were planning a bit of cake and coffee, and she hoped that I would stay. She also knew what had happened on my last visit and that Candice didn't want me around.

When Candice came down, she immediately said, "What are you doing here?"

I replied, "Came to celebrate your birthday!"

"You didn't have to do that" was her cold response.

"But I want to," I said. "It even rained the day you were born."

"No, it didn't," she yelled. "You don't know when I was born. You are not my dad." And then she said, "You are Dun Vandonken [that is the name she uses for me, must come from one of her voices], not my dad," and then yelled at everyone seated around. "He is bad. Don't talk to him." The lady in charge interrupted and asked Candice to open her card and read it to everyone. She did that in a very irritated fashion and then looking at me, took the money, put it in her pocket, and said, "You didn't need to do that."

One of the women then called out to her, "Hon, give your father a hug."

In a very loud voice, she said, "No, he is bad." She then screamed at me, "Get out and never come back."

I couldn't help but start to cry. She asked, "What are you doing?"

"Crying," I replied. My eyes were filled with tears.

She got up, walked toward me talking more loudly, "Get out! Get out!" So I got up and left. I did not want to put those women, all of whom are in some way disabled, through any more of that kind of experience.

It was a scene I can't forget. I keep thinking of her as that bright, smart, able young girl who was the apple of my eye. She was so advanced in many ways—loved music, always had a big smile, was a superb athlete and scholar with a perfect report card. I remember thinking to myself as I used to kiss her good night, *If anything ever happens to her, I will be devastated.* Those thoughts and that terrible scene just keep tumbling back and forth in my head.

The worst part is that I don't have you with whom to weep. As soon as I got into the car, I called Karen and told her the story, still crying. And she began to cry, saying, "I'm so sorry, Dad." She felt guilty because she didn't feel well enough to go with me. She continues to struggle with anxiety about what is causing her inability to swallow and stomach discomfort. It all caused me to feel so alone and depressed. I guess I may need to seek a counselor. I do have some friends to whom I could talk but just don't feel that closeness necessary to unburden myself. I know part of my problem is not willing to make myself vulnerable.

Sometimes I think I made the wrong decision coming back to church in Pompton Plains, spent too long there wearing a leader's gown and not able to reflect my need for love and healing, not blaming any friend I have made but more my unwillingness to be vulnerable. I know I'm feeling a bit sorry for myself right now and will get beyond it. I always have lived knowing tomorrow is the home of hope. So I go on, but I really miss you through this.

Thanks for being such a wonderful wife and soul mate.

Many hugs and kisses!

A Dinner Date with Charlie and Jenny

Dear Mae,

I had dinner with Charlie and Jenny tonight at Nicola's in Totowa. We used to go there occasionally. We had cousin Andrew Wood's repast there. I always liked that restaurant. The food is excellent. Seating is comfortable, and the noise is minimal, so conversation is very possible. It is also a BOB (bring your bottle), and we enjoyed a couple glasses of wine. You would have had your Kailua.

It was good being with them since we haven't really spent much time together this summer. It won't be long till they will be back on their way to Florida. Jenny seems to be doing well, but Charlie is having some health issues. He is experiencing sudden onslaughts of sweating, and they can't determine the cause. He has been taking various tests and will find out the results in a couple of days. He hardly ate his meal, a pasta dish. He also is quite thin, but then he never was heavy. We spent much of the evening talking about my concerns over Candice and Karen. Karen is improving with the help of a holistic doctor, but the situation with Candice remains the same. And although I know there is nothing I can do, it is good to talk to people who are familiar with her situation and the struggles we have had over the years. This brought up many memories of our years as friends. We talked of our skiing days and how we had said we wanted to ski until we were ninety. Well, that was wishful thinking! We laughed about how you were so speedy on the hills, and we gave you the nickname "Ms. Jehu." We remembered all the wonderful trips to ski resorts we took together. We surely had a privileged life.

One of our enjoyable memories was the time I picked up a bushel of crabs on the way home from Dover AFB, probably in 1976. You had someone take a picture of us—you, me, and Jenny sitting at the kitchen table in Clifton holding a crab. The year before you died, you posted it on Facebook, and recently it reappeared and prompted all kinds of responses. Remember how that kitchen smelled for a couple of days? It didn't make you a happy camper.

I also talked about how both Charlie and I are getting hearing aids. Finally decided to get them. Charlie has had them for a while. He says his are working well, although he is still not used to wearing them. I am looking forward to getting mine in ten days. Hearing things on TV and in a theatre have all become difficult. I also have trouble hearing Kathleen preach. When her voice reaches a pitch, it escapes me. We talked about what Charlie likes and doesn't about them. I am looking forward to giving them a try. I bought them at Costco, and if they don't work for me in the first six months I can return, and get my money back. So I shall see! I am positive you would like it because you often complained about me not hearing what you said. Was this selective on my part, or did I really not hear you? That we will never know!

Good night, honey. I am going to get ready for bed. I sure missed you tonight. It is not the same, even kind of awkward, being one person having dinner with friends who are a couple, just have to keep learning how to live and enjoy life as a single person. I do have a tendency to avoid these kinds of events, but I know it is necessary to keep on developing social contacts. It would be worse to avoid, but without you, I am tempted.

Hugs and hugs and hugs!

Hearing Aids

Hi, honey.

Today I am making a retiree chaplain visit to a new retiree in Pompton Lakes. It is a female, and I don't know if she is married. I was just notified by the Board of Benefits that she was retired and in my area. I am going to meet her at a restaurant. I offered to visit her place, but she said she lives at the parsonage in Wanaque and was not anxious for me to come there. I tell you all this because it will be my first visit with the new hearing aids, anxious to discover how they function in a restaurant conversation with other noise all around. That has been a problem for me. The noise in the restaurant competes with the conversation.

Getting the briefing on how to wear, clean, and store them was sort of stressful. But then it seems like most things are because I am increasingly feeling alone, and that heightens my feeling of vulnerability First of all, I had to take the small earpieces in my hands and open and close the place where the battery sits. The battery especially, but also the aids are far smaller than what I am able to handle easily. Because of the neuropathy which came about from the stem cell transplant and chemo, it is very difficult to feel with the tips of my fingers. It is getting most difficult to even fasten buttons on shirts. I need you to help me. Holding the aids and pulling them apart to insert a battery had me on edge. I definitely will have to do this over a towel and in a place with lots of light in case I drop them and they accidentally fall on the floor, where, because of the size and color of the battery, I won't find them.

The lesson on how to clean them was especially difficult because a small brush must be used each morning to clean off the wax dust that builds up at night in the dryer where they are placed after wear. There is also a need for cleaning wax from the interior of the device about once a year, or more often if hearing is diminished. This is done by pulling off the nipple that enters the ear and using an instrument (very small) to poke in a hole (also very small) on the interior of the small unit. I tried it a couple times with the tutelage of the technician, and although I did it, I'm not sure if I could do it again by myself. I may have to return for help.

The real neat thing was that it is possible to sync the units with my iPhone. I can use the phone to increase or decrease volume and can also answer phone calls through the aids without having the phone in the same room. I would guess it has to be in the same building some place, but not necessarily on my person. Although I am wearing them today for this appointment, I didn't wear them yesterday when golfing. I don't think it is a good idea to wear them during any physical activity like golf, and definitely not swimming, of course!

Well, I wore them for lunch and now my report. I hated them. I couldn't get them adjusted so I could hear this soft-speaking lady, and wouldn't you know it, a pair of loud speaking men took the table next to us. I heard them better than the lady. It was a very frustrating experience. I was up front with her and told her what I was experiencing, and like most pastors, she was very understanding. As soon as I got home, I took them out and enjoyed the evening without hearing aids and asked myself why I decided to purchase them.

Today I went to lunch with Enid. We do this every six weeks or so, and as she puts it, we remember the wonderful dinners we had together with our departed spouses. We laugh often about things that either you or Tippy said on occasions we recall. Anyway, today I wore those hearing aids again, and we found a place in the restaurant where it was quiet. So they did not bother me as much. I also turned them down which I can do with the iPhone. I felt better about them. But at dinner time, Mary Peterson called. And since they were synced with the phone, I could not hear her, and she couldn't hear me. I had to take them out so we could have a conversation. I will need to find out how to make that feature work, or otherwise I will need to disconnect from the phone. I do have six months to determine if they are right for me. I will give them a good test.

There is another topic that I am prompted to write about tonight. But it is too late, and I am tired. It needs a whole letter, so I will make it a future subject. So long for this day, another warm and rainy early October day, not too long before I will be reflecting on the reality that I lost you four years ago. Monday is Columbus Day, and that was D-day. But it isn't the thirteenth this year as it was in 2014. I get to mourn your loss twice, on Columbus Day and on the date you were killed—the thirteenth.

My love for you will never fade, hugs and kisses.

Fourth Anniversary

—— ⌘ ——

Dear Mae,

Today marks four years since your fatal accident. It is a gloomy day as it should be, dark and rainy. I had a hard time getting out of bed. I slept almost eight hours last night, straight through. When I finally awoke, the first thought was of you and how I wished we could go to breakfast together. I remember how going out to breakfast was not your favorite, but because I liked it, you always accompanied me. Karen was also aware, as was Richelle. She called last night and reminded me of the date. Karen listed a number of things on Facebook today. The one picture she posted was of you and Pat dressed in the outfits of the Roaring Twenties standing next to a model T in the driveway of Grace Manse. You just loved doing those crazy things, and it's one of the reasons I loved you so much. You were always filled with surprises.

Karen also posted this quote from Rose Kennedy which was so appropriate for the day and how we felt: "It has been said, 'Time heals all wounds.' I do not agree. The wounds remain. In time, the mind, protecting its sanity covers them with scar tissue and the pain lessens. But it is never gone!" So true! I feel the pain just gets different all the time. The pain remains, and sometimes it gets more severe than expected.

I had lunch with Rett on Friday. Of course, much of our talk centered around our grieving, him because of Astride and me because of you. It is good talking with him. He has a healthy perspective and helps me keep mine. Astride has been gone eleven years, hard

80

to believe it happened seven years before your accident. I remember going to a celebration of her life at Wyckoff Church and how we talked on the way home as to how we would respond if an accidental death like hers ever happened to either of us.

Back to the anniversary day. Karen invited me there for dinner. She did her best to make a nice meal and prepare a time to appreciate each other, but it was ever apparent that your chair was empty. I do appreciate being there at times like that. Karen prepared a big plate of crackers with smoked salmon and a glass of good red wine. Stella smelled the salmon, and she kept bothering me, and I had to protect the plate from her. She seems to treat me with a special affection, almost seems aware that you should really be with me when visiting—brings back memories of our dog sitting her and Tori when the family went on vacation.

I stayed around until about nine thirty. I don't really like to drive at night anymore, and since I had a glass and half of wine, I waited before leaving and was very careful on the way home. I did not sleep well. I woke up about 4:00 a.m. and didn't get back to sleep until about six o'clock. I slept for an hour and then got up for church. It was the end to a strange week. Since Monday was Columbus Day and I was reminded of your loss on that day, the morose feelings sort of lingered for the whole week. Only Karen and I were in church since everyone else had stuff going on. So even the start of the new week didn't feel quite right.

Last night, Bev called, and that helped. She and Dave were on their way home from Syracuse where they were with their son Phillip and were also with Jane Style. She remembered the date and called to express her and David's love. They are planning to be in New Jersey this week to visit David's brother who is quite sick. I invited them to stay here, or at least stop in to see my place. Because she was such a close friend with you, she was also affected by the commemoration of the date. I told her that if they can't stop, I will see them in Michigan. I am going to fly out a week from tomorrow and stay for a week. I don't want to drive there anymore. Driving alone seems too dangerous at this age. If you were still here, I would drive. You always were such a helpmate as we traveled. Although you were never a back-seat driver, you always made a trip pleasant.

Enough for now! Ever grateful we had so many wonderful years together!

Love ya.

Dinner with Bev, Dave, and Karen

Hi, hon.

When Dave and Bev got to New Jersey, Bev called and wondered when we could get together. We made a date for Saturday noon, lunch and a view of my condo and complex. I invited Karen to come over and enjoy their visit as well. When they got to my place and entered the condo, Bev's first words were my first thought when I saw the model, "Mae would love this." They were very impressed and expressed their happiness that I have this wonderful place to live. I also showed them the clubhouse and pools. We went to lunch at a restaurant that I have come to like a lot, The Quiet Man, in Dover on Route 46. It is hardly what the name conveys. It's noisy, especially near the bar. It is an Irish pub and more. Cal Heerschap took me there the first time, and I have gone there with friends since.

We enjoyed a nice lunch and shared a lot of memories in addition to catching up. Recently Bev fell and broke her right elbow, so she has been out of commission for about six weeks. She will resume working with Ken next week when they will be doing some work in Grand Rapids. Since I am going to visit my family in Grand Rapids, we will get together again and perhaps go to one of the concerts he is giving at the old Christian High where Jeanne, Rusty, and Ken attended. Ken is doing a benefit for a federation that is reshaping the building to make it multiuse for community youth programs.

I tell you this because I know how much you loved and appreciated these people and how excited you would be being with them and attending such a concert. We talked together at lunch about how you and them played so many tricks on each other, how you and Bev went into the city for college classes, and how you were always wanting to pick up trash and cans in the gutter to clean up the city. You had such a high sense of responsibility for caring for the environment. You would be livid about our present president's cavalier attitude toward environmental issues, and so much more, but I want to devote an entire letter to that.

I am finishing this letter after returning from Michigan. I planned on writing while I was there but kept involved so much of the time I didn't get anything on the computer. It was kind of a sad visit because we always made this visit together. I really miss you sleeping in that big bed Jeanne bought hoping that this would attract us to Michigan more often. I know she misses you as well because she invariably makes remarks about how you did and said things when we were here together. Now that her dog is gone, she did very little walking until recently. She and her neighbor, Marilyn, now go to a fitness center, a very good decision on her part.

The day I arrived in Michigan, my brothers, their wives, and Jeanne met for a late lunch or early dinner at Rainbow Grill in Hudsonville. Rachael was also present. She spent a week with John and Marti prior to my arrival. She is looking for work. Her gig with *Wildlife Docs* is finished. Too bad! It was a great show, and she was very good as the hostess. On Monday, John and Marti left for Sedona for the winter. Jeanne and I attended LaGrave Church Sunday where we met people I knew and also knew you as well. For dinner, we had pot roast at Carol's father's home, and I shared with him the news that he was one of the persons who had an influence on my decision to write these letters. For ninety-four, he is in great physical shape, and his mind is equally sharp. Carol did the cooking, and in the afternoon, we celebrated her sister Nancy's birthday. Carol's other two sisters stopped by later, and we had cake.

We were also able to spend some more time with Ken and Bev, enjoyed dinner on Monday night, minus Dave because he wasn't feeling well. Unfortunately, Dave's issues with Crohn's disease kicked up. Thinking of Dave's problem, I couldn't help thinking about how you dealt with Crohn's. You were so intent on finding the best way of coping and not taking medication. I often wonder how things would have gone during those four years since your death. If you had remained alive, would you be as healthy as you were and as able to deal with the Crohn's by just managing your diet? When I realize how uncomfortable David becomes with his attacks, I am grateful for you and I do not have to face that part of our life together. (Incidentally David had surgery, and it has been very successful. He is doing well.) I say "our" because I always felt stressed when you were uncomfortable. I wanted to do something to help, wanted to clear up your discomfort, and there was no way to do it.

I'm going to close this letter. I want to start a fresh one on the celebration of All Saints Sunday we had yesterday. As you can imagine, you were the focus of my thoughts.

Love.

All Saints Sunday

—— ✍ ——

Morning, hon.

I am sure you remember an "All Saints Sunday" celebration we had at Pompton Plains after Pastor Kathleen arrived. I don't think we worshipped there often on All Saints Sunday, but I think there was at least once we both attended. Little candles were provided which were lit and then placed in a tray on a table even as worshippers go forward for communion. We did it again yesterday, and I found it quite meaningful, at least thought-provoking. Karen and Karlee were with me. Bruce and Garrett had gone to Pennsylvania for the day. Just the three of us went forward: my daughter, granddaughter, both of whom resemble you so much, and me.

The thought that hit as we were singing was what a saint you were. Through all the cancer, bone marrow transplant, and surgery, you were always as close as you could be to make sure that I was comfortable and in the process of healing. I remember you saying often, "You have only one job now, and that is to get well." You did all you could to make that possible, not only in physical care, but in the enormous emotional and spiritual support you provided. As I was reflecting with tears in my eyes, we were singing "For All the Saints." Most of the day, I did a lot of thinking about our relationship and what I miss the most. This is my conclusion: it is the freedom and opportunity to be totally vulnerable which you made possible.

Richard Rohr wrote this in this morning's devotional,

> I think most people are called to marriage because we need at least one other person to be like a mirror for us, to reflect our best self—and our worst self—in a way that we can receive. The interesting thing about a mirror is that it doesn't change the image; it simply takes it in as it is. Our closest friends or life partner hold a mirror up to us, revealing our good side and our dark side and reminding us that we still haven't really learned to love. That's what every healthy relationship does. (Devotion entitled "Love," November 5, 2018)

Our relationship did that for me. It made me feel like I could be fully who I am with you. There were no charades. I didn't have to put on with you, and if I did, you caught me. Of course, it wasn't always that way. It is what our relationship became, and once having experienced such a wonderful bond, there is no way to replicate.

I met Gabe and Shiela (friends of ours at Shawnee Golf Club) in Costco last week. As we talked about a number of things, they asked if any other woman has come into my life. I replied that I have had some dinner dates and have some women friends but then said that after a fifty-five-year marriage to a person who so identified with me and I with her, there is no way I can see trying to build a new relationship; and at this age, I don't have the energy or desire to try. I fear that in time, any new relationship at my age would become more a burden than a pleasure for both partners.

I don't know if people can understand this. Gabe and Sheila are on their second marriage, and from all I sense, it is very good. But they divorced and remarried when they were much younger and at a time when their previous relationships were hardly what ours had become. I guess some of the feeling I had in church was that there will never be anything like it again, and that is sad. But even in this sadness, I can hope and believe that God is ever making all things new, takes me back to the rainbow image Bonnie sent me when she heard of your death while in China.

I guess the big fear I have in taking this rather independent stance about a new relationship is that as I face the reality of a body breaking down with age, I will miss having anyone close enough to go through this with me. This is the challenge each widow or widower faces, and with great angst, as the clock ticks. We need to think about this and make appropriate plans but not allow it to overwhelm us. I definitely want to guard against that!

I am happy that we had some good talks about this during the last years of your life. It helped me deal with the reality of your loss when it occurred. One of the first thoughts among a myriad of them that raced through my brain when the state police woman gave me the bad news was, *Well, we knew it would come one day to one of us. Now I have to get on with a different kind of living.* And so I have, and I don't like it a lot of the time. But the experiences of the years and times we enjoyed together overwhelm all other memories. We had some tough times, some real disagreements, some moments of anger with each other; but those memories are very weak, hardly real!

Now to get to making a good supper, I'm preparing a spinach salad with bacon, hard-boiled egg, small portobello mushrooms, and some red onions. I need to figure out a tasty dressing. I wish we could enjoy it together. Love ya, hon!

The Election

Good morning, honey.

Since you departed, a lot of things have transpired in the world of politics, and I want to talk with you about some of it. You and I were always quite interested in the lives and views of people involved in politics and government on both the local and national scene. We had some strong bias and were pretty much in lockstep on most social issues. I especially remember our Miami days when we were "Religious Observers" at the Republican and Democratic National Conventions held on Miami Beach. It was educational, exhilarating, and exciting. We had so many close-up views of many principal participants, party delegates, and journalists. The big issue on our minds at that time was how the country could be saved from the disaster that took place in Chicago at the democratic convention in 1968. As a Miami clergy fellowship, we designed the concept of "Religious Observers" who would be present at both conventions hopefully to de-escalate any kind of serious confrontation between protestors and delegates. We both enjoyed many conversations on the streets with people of both parties and did our best to converse without causing conflict and promote better understanding

Because of those memories, I would like to hear how you would feel about our present president, Donald Trump. His election has ignited a rather toxic political culture where people are either vehemently opposed to him or ardently supportive. He made a statement during the campaign that he could shoot a person on Broadway, and people would still support him. Perhaps that is one of the most accurate statements he has made. In many ways, he is reminiscent of Nixon who was the center of so much controversy back in 1972. His style and verbal expressions tend to divide communities, churches, families, and friends. Many are finding it very difficult to have open political discussions. In our building, when the men meet together for coffee or breakfast, political discussion is off limits. When someone even slightly broaches a political subject, the whole crowd warns not to go there. There is even a difference of opinion in our family which has caused some uncomfortable discussions. You would have been very upset over much of this public dispute and probably keep silent, but bristle inside, because of your usual desire for peace and tranquility.

Most of the conservative, evangelical Christian community supports Trump as a protector of the American way, difficult for me to accept. Although I cherish the freedom we enjoy and served in the military to support those who defended our country, I am troubled with our national obsession for power and economic control. Trump's clarion call is that America must be great, which I consider a very uncharitable way of seeing ourselves in respect to the rest of the world. I want America to be caring, just, honest, peaceful, and very aware of so many who have much less than us and be willing to commit to help. It seems to me that the goal of America being great doesn't develop the kind of culture that creates a more caring and just world.

I just needed to let off steam in this letter, releasing frustration at having to hear so many people I love and appreciate take what I consider such a materialistic approach to the political scene. As I age, I become more alert to the reality that we are living in a spiritual vacuum, even much more since losing you. I feel strongly that the president, although not solely responsible, contributes inordinately. One of your cousins commented on Facebook that it didn't matter about Trump's sexual activity or his moral behavior, we should be happy he is president because there are more jobs and a better economy. Excuse the pun, but does a better economy "trump" basic moral values?

Well, enough of this. Knowing you as I did, I am sure you would have feelings and thoughts that are similar. I have decided that I can't keep quiet and not reveal that I don't fully support his presidency. I am not going to disrespect him as a leader. I will support those things that he does that are productive for the common good and praise him for those. If people ask why I do not support him fully, I will simply invite them to read the Sermon on the Mount (Matthew 5–7) reflectively, asking the question, how do these words of Jesus relate to our nation today?

Thanks for hearing out my rant. Anyway, I hope you sense my pain about this. I so miss how freely we could share these expressions together and even converse with friends who disagreed and for whom we had respect and could carry on quality relationships. It just doesn't seem this is possible right now, but everything does change in time. I remain ever hopeful. I am sure you would see all this with much less angst than me. Love you, darling!

"Our days as religious observers at the Democratic and Republican conventions in Miami Beach 1972. How much we enjoyed talking to all of those people and at times helped to prevent conflict among delegates."

A Real Tough Weekend

Dear Mazy,

Remember when Pat Hellyer would call you "bargain basement Mazy?" I think you really appreciated it because you were always very thrifty and proud of it, and I was proud of you as well. You would have been happy with me this weekend. I stayed home and didn't spend any money and decided to do a few things around the condo like taking out recycles and sorting some more clothes and other items to give away. Also, the weather was miserable, cold rain. Staying in was the most attractive option. However, in the process of it all, I hurt myself. The door that opens our trash room is very heavy and difficult to pull open with nothing else in your hands. Well, I decided to pull it open with a basket of recyclables in my hands. The door slammed against my back and bumped me into the wall with my left arm and elbow banging into the chair rail, and it began to bleed rather heavily.

This in itself is bad enough, but now that I am taking Eliquis, which is a drug that thins the blood and prevents strokes and is necessary because of my AFib, bleeding was heavy. This drug prevents blood clots so one needs to be careful with an open wound. Bleeding can be difficult to stop, and I was worried. Immediately I looked for bandaging materials, and when I found them, it was very difficult to prepare for placement on the elbow and keeping it from bleeding too heavily. Because my surgically repaired right shoulder allows little flexibility, I could hardly reach the elbow. After some extreme effort and a very poorly prepared bandage, I did get the blood stopped and decided that I would keep it that way for the rest of the day and even at night in bed.

The bleeding ceased; but the whole time, I was lamenting not having you around, not just to help with a bandage but for emotional support. Those are the ways we would assist each other, particularly you for me. I always depended on you to wash off wounds and bind them up which you took on with even more resolve after all my cancer episodes. The following morning, I knew I had to remove the bandage and did only to discover that it was bleeding again because the bandage had stuck to the scar and tore it open. My immediate decision was to head to a walk-in clinic not more than five minutes away. When I arrived, the woman at the desk was on the phone. Simply keeping the phone in her hand, she gave me papers to fill out. The bleeding was continuing because I had again made a very poor temporary bandage. I asked if they could dress the wound. Yes, but I must first fill out the papers—seven sheets. Looking at them, I noted that the information they wanted was already in my doctor's records and had to be in the Atlantic Health System since that is my doctor's system. Makes no difference, I needed to fill it out. In the process, I needed to list Karen as a person to be notified. And in looking up her number on the phone, I accidentally called, and Bruce answered. "Do I need them to come up?" he asked.

"No," I said, "Didn't mean to call, just looking for your number." And I explained where I was and why. I tried to continue filling out the forms and discovered they wanted all my medications, all medical history, all of which was in the system; and when I told this to the woman, she said that nonetheless, I had to fill it out because this walk-in clinic demands a separate posting. Around this time, I was really getting very upset. I told her I am not filling it out and that I am going to leave. As I leave, Karen called and said she was on her way up and would wrap the wound. I guess Bruce sensed something in my voice that indicated I needed help and told Karen, and she decided to come. I was able to restrict the bleeding enough to get home, and shortly after, Karen arrived. She did a very nice job of cleaning and wrapping the wound. It is at such times I feel so all alone and also that I am too far from where Karen and Bruce live.

Part of this loneliness is associated with the growing weakness related to aging. My shoulder hurts and doesn't function normally, and my legs feel weaker. Just getting up and down steps is an action that demands total focus so I don't slip and fall. If only you were here. You would at least give me the comfort of your presence and encouragement, and of course, take care of bleeding. I also think of how much worse it might have been for you if I had died first. Women can feel even more vulnerable.

Yesterday, when I went for mail, I met Eddy, a woman living in my building whose husband died a couple months ago. She began to tell me about her two adult children who were caught in the early snowstorm we had on Thursday that came quickly and heavy at peak travel time. Traffic was a mess, and there were accidents all over the area. Route 80 was closed west bound. It took them hours to get from New York City. She knew they were in that traffic and was frightened. As I listened, I was prompted to ask how she was doing generally; and she began to relate how scared she is now living alone, how she has removed herself from Facebook for fear of contacts people may make with her. She fears answering the phone because of all the strange calls received on a regular basis. It was apparent in her voice and eyes that she was speaking the truth. I told her that if she ever needed to talk, I would be ready to listen. I got to know her just following the move here. When her husband got sick, I visited him in a rehab center, and the whole family was present. They are a practicing Catholic family, and I had a prayer with them. I think she shared with me because she felt I could provide some spiritual encouragement. Anyway, she made me keenly aware of how much lonelier and more frightened a single aging woman can be who has lost her mate: a strong and vital guy.

Well, this letter is getting longer than usual, but the parts about Eddy came to mind because of my thoughts on being all alone. And before I sign off, I want to finish about the weekend which accented my feelings of loneliness. Karen left about noon. We took time together to look at some things I have put away which I want her to be aware of in case anything happens, like a safety deposit box key, financial records, and some important papers. Once she was gone, I went into the fridge to get something to eat. I hadn't taken time to eat, and I was hungry. Perhaps I moved too quickly opening the door because the unopened plastic jar of V8 juice in the rack of the door fell out on the floor. The plastic cap broke and three fourths of the contents spilled all over. What a total mess!

Who was going to clean it up? This liquid could not stay on this kind of flooring very long! It would ruin it. I can't get down on my knees any longer because I can hardly get up, also, tough to bend over! What do I do? Here is where you always dove in and took over and found a way to clean it up promptly and with relative ease. Only occasionally would you complain. Well, I did it. With energy and strength I didn't think I had, I used cloth towels, paper towels, a swifter mop with wet covers and got it cleaned up! Later, I washed all the towels in the washer, along with the pants I was wearing which were splashed up to the knees with V8 juice. I took off my shoes and socks which also had to be washed.

Hon, I really don't know how I am going to continue to carry on without you, but I will! These episodes indicate I can do it, but oh, it is so difficult without you! We never fully know when we had one another how much we need and depend on each other. Anyway, you meant so much to me, and the wonderful memories live on.

Love ya!

Article

Good day before Thanksgiving! I will have Bruce, Karen, and the grandkids over for Thanksgiving. They are going into New York City to see the parade and then come here for dinner. Today, I am sending you part of an article I had published this fall in a pamphlet entitled *In Touch*. I am sure you recall. It is put out by the Board of Benefits. Anyway, it consists of articles written by Reformed church pastors describing their years of retirement. While you were still alive, I didn't feel motivated to write one; but this spring, I got the urge.

I began the article by mentioning our interim time in South Bend at the Christian Reformed Church. Then I told of becoming aware of my non-Hodgkin's cancer while doing an interim at Nutley Reformed Church. I related how difficult the time was following Nutley since I had to undergo a bone marrow transplant. I still think almost weekly about those days and how attentive you were to my needs.

In the next part of the article, I described your sudden death and how that loss affected me. The part of the article I want to include is what describes how I feel now after your death and all the changes of buying a condo, moving back to New Jersey, and reconnecting with so many friends.

There has been much heartache because of such a loss, but it also has made me more aware of how we need to see this last part of life as a time for giving up those things and even persons, who have been so important to us. It is a time to prepare ourselves for the greater adventure God has mostly kept as a mystery to challenge our faith. It is a time to disengage and rid ourselves of much of the stuff that we worked so hard to accumulate. Living without the one I loved so much makes me more aware of how little value there is to all the things we valued so much as we grew older together. Stuff that we gathered, investments we managed, homes that we cherished, toys that entertained us, even the people who touched us in so many wonderful ways, including our children and grandchildren, need to become less that we may be prepared for that fuller relationship with the greater presence of the Spirit of God we anticipate by faith.

Some of my present joys are the opportunities I have to share my story with those who struggle so significantly to survive tough losses we all endure as we journey through this life to one day achieve the greater life that God has for us. I guess in all this I have been trying to say that my retirement, as pleasant and as disheartening as it has been, has also largely been preparing me for the end, and that is good! I am ready, but I plan to live as vigorously as I am able until the "bell tolls."

I have received and still am receiving a number of positive responses. I thought it was appropriate to include this on the fifth Thanksgiving without you. I am very grateful for the wonderful years we enjoyed together and especially the sensitive and almost omnipresent care you gave during the tough days of the bone-marrow transplant. I will always remember that with much gratitude and love.

Karen, Bruce, and the grandchildren went to the parade in New York City and enjoyed it, although the temperature was in the teens.

While they were there, I picked up a preordered turkey dinner from Wegmans supermarket. It was a fourteen pounder with mashed potatoes, stuffing, gravy, a string bean casserole, butternut squash, and cranberry sauce. It was all cooked and packed. All I had to do was place it in the oven and reheat. Clear instructions were provided. It turned out to be delicious, and all the preparation was done for us. I felt good being able to host the family. Of course, we were very conscious of the empty chair and your organizing ability to get it all ready. You may not have done all the cooking when we hosted, but you did the table setting in your special way and organized things that we would have all the food ready to serve and enjoy while it was warm. Again, you were very much missed.

Love you so!

Andrew

The Christmas Letter

Good afternoon, hon.

It's a strange week, trying to get ready for Christmas, which involves getting out our year-end letter, shopping for Christmas presents, having Karen help me do some decorating, and keeping dates for lunch with a number of people. The big thing has been the Christmas letter. I really did not want to write it this year. I haven't been taking any pictures to include in such a letter; and I didn't want to put down a list of things that have happened this year, the trips I took, and the time in Florida of which I had no pictures. I just did not have the energy to do it.

Well, just as I had made up my mind not to write, I got a phone call from John Holwerda. I won't say anymore. Here is the letter.

> A grateful Christmas and a challenging 2019 to all!
>
> It is almost the end of another year! Time to send the Rienstra year-end letter. After all we have done it as long as I can remember. Mae took the initiative. Wrote cute, clever quips that went along with pictures of family artfully placed in sequential order. Now I must do it....and I don't want to! Everything ends somewhere!! Quit preaching this year, stopped driving to Michigan to visit family, no more car trips to Florida for winter breaks. It's done!

"No, I am not sending out a letter this year," I said to myself as I laid in bed on a cold rainy morning last week…and then the phone rang. It was John, an old college buddy whom I may have seen a dozen times since graduation in 1956. He has also phoned me about 20 times in those 62 years. In his boisterous, jocular voice he asks how I am doing. All kinds of memories pop into my head. He tells me he was thinking of me and how I must be doing without Mae. He doesn't know how he would survive without his wife…and we go on and on talking about a zillion things. As abruptly as he began our conversation, he ended it by instructing me to look up a poem on the internet, "The Cookie Thief." After he hung up, I had an idea he would be calling another of our old buddies to provide his unique and kind, caring encouragement.

The call got me thinking about all the splendid, special people who have shown up in my life. Some are no longer here. They left to be with Mae, my parents and many others in God's new adventure. Others are like you, people who touched me as John, encouraged me when most needed. His call was a reminder to be more grateful for the many of you who have enriched my journey. So… I decided to write this letter anyway! I want to thank you for being you, for the unique way you affected me and our family through the years. You may have never realized that as John, it was the little thing you did, the smile, the hug, the phone call, the kind word even the challenging words to get off the "pity pot" that made a difference at the right time. You were the Spirit of what Christmas is all about. Thanks!

And more…continue to encourage each other. A writer I read recently made this unusual point. Rather than making all this fuss about keeping Christ in Christmas, keep Herod in Christmas. Herod in Christmas? The ruthless king who killed babies? Yes, when it appears it can't get any worse, remember and trust in the baby who was born at just the right time. He waits again this Christmas to be born anew in those who make a difference by sharing love, hope and peace. I know! I've experienced his coming to life in so many of you! Thanks again!

Love you all,
Andy

Once I had it written, I had to print it and to do so, decided to purchase a nonbrand colored ink. I wanted to print it in green and red. Ink for this printer is not cheap. As you always advised, find the most economical way to purchase ink. Remember we used to get empty cartridges refilled at Costco? I did find cheap ink. A website had ink for less than half it would cost if I purchased the ink HP advised for the printer. It arrived in two days, and I started printing using special paper purchased from Staples as we regularly did. It all began well. Green ink worked just fine and looked great, complemented nicely the various shades of red decorations on the paper. Suddenly, it appeared the printer ran out of ink. I struggled to determine the reason and discovered the printer heads were clogged, and in trying to rectify the situation, ink spilled all over the printer. It was a mess! I had to use all kinds of paper towels to clean it. To sum it up, I had to buy the HP ink anyway. The fellow at Staples said that this often happens when people use the cheaper ink because they are refilled cartridges that have smaller holes. After some very aggravating hours, the letter got printed and sent. I'm not sure I will do this again—next year, only e-mail letters to contacts.

Why weren't you here to help? Writing the letter was no problem. Getting it sent out with all the decorations and pictures was your job. Again, how I missed you!

Love you, hon!

Our Discussions, Really Arguments

Dear Mae,

It is time to go to bed, and I do feel tired, but want to connect and talk about some of the events of the day. I finally had a decent sleep last night and woke up refreshed. I have been bothered with stuffed nostrils and can't breathe through my nose. I finally decided to use Afrin even though the doctor advises against it. It does seem to clear things up so I can breathe. Once I got up, I had to move quickly because of an appointment for the usual nine weeks shot in my eye for the retinal problems. The first thing I usually do every morning, after making the bed and getting a cup of coffee, is check e-mail. In it was a response to some e-mail I had sent Tom Larkin. I sent him the first letter written to you to give him an idea of what this project is all about. Here is what he wrote.

> Hi Andy,
>
> I could not recall if I responded to your sending these letters to Mae. Thank you very much for sending the letters. There are many others I believe you have written as well. Hope and pray, others may read them and be helped in some way in their grieving. Not only in grieving but living life more fully in faith and trust.
> My life (speaking for Linda and Thomas too) has been blessed by you & Mae and will be

always grateful to our Lord that our paths crossed. I still remember being in a car with both of you, and you & Mae had a heated discussion while I observed in the back seat, forgot the topic. Even in your different opinions, and each of you had some very strong views, your love for each other was very evident.

Just read your Christmas letter. Your concluding note about keeping Herod in Christmas I found helpful, and insightful.

A blessed Christmas to you and your family my dear friend and mentor.

In peace, joy, and love,
Tom (Linda and Thomas)

I was struck by his remark about our "heated discussion," the time he was in the back seat of our car. It made me smile. We often had those heated discussions, and we were not afraid who listened in on them. It makes me think that it was one of the strengths of our relationship. We disagreed on many things, and we were never afraid to let each other know. But as Tom observed, it was always done in a spirit of loving each other. We might have been quite angry with each other at times, but it never distracted from our love. I think it enriched it! We just had strong views about many aspects of living. And as Tom said, we expressed them, and it never diminished our love for each other.

I really think that was one of the strengths of our marriage, a willingness to engage in open discussion about any number of topics on which we agreed and disagreed. There is much that I miss in losing you, and one that I think about often is that there is no longer anyone to really get upset with and have a good argument. The women friends I have offer an opportunity for conversation and a measure of companionship, but there is no one I feel close enough with to have a good drag-out argument. I really miss that!

It makes me think of some of the marriage counseling I did. So many couples either argued out of a real sense of dislike for the other or for the purpose of changing the other person, or they didn't argue at all. They kept everything locked tight inside and bred resentment and deeper anger.

I can't help thinking that some of the depression I feel associated with your loss is that there are subjects I want to discuss and even argue about, and there is no one I feel close enough to engage, comes to mind especially at this season. It seemed like we always got into some type of tussle preparing for Christmas. It would often start with setting up and decorating the Christmas tree, even purchasing it at times, and then there were the presents we intended to purchase, the food and drinks to serve at our parties, the people to invite, and I could go on and on. Things would get complicated, and yet in the end, we always had a wonderful time and celebration and became ever more appreciative of each other.

Writing this, I am reminded of the Christmas parties we had for the church staff at the manse. Kathleen is having an open house at the manse this Sunday. Sister Jeanne will be here and will appreciate being able to see the manse once again. I don't think she has been there since we moved out. It will be interesting to hear her reaction. One of the things Kathleen does is refer to the manse as her home, which of course it is as it was ours when we lived there. She just is not as sensitive to how some people let us know that they wanted us to refer to it as "Friendly Manse." Maybe it was because she didn't know Pat Hellyer as we did, and that makes me smile.

I started this letter late. I just got off a phone call from Wes Kort, and it stimulated me to want to write, but now it's time for beddy-bye. If you were here, you would probably still be wide awake doing things to get our home and life ready for Christmas. You were the best!

Love ya.

Christmas at Karen's

Dearest Mae,

Ever since you left us, I have celebrated Christmas at Karen and Bruce's home. We also did so again yesterday with sister Jeanne, Bruce's sister Sue, her husband, Korky, and daughter, Sarah, also Josh, Garrett, and Karlee. Of all the times (it's been five now), this seemed best for me. I can't give a definitive reason. How I feel living without you seems to change just like that. One minute I feel okay, and a moment later, I am in tears for no reason. A thought just comes to mind, and the tear ducts open. A woman in my building who lost her husband this summer said the same thing to me as we exchanged pleasantries a couple days ago. She said one day it seems okay and normal, and the next she feels horrible. I think that kind of roller coaster is going to continue for the rest of my life.

Anyway, yesterday was fairly good for Christmas Day. I did quite a bit of work putting all the presents in bags I had purchased. I always depended on you to do the wrapping. I always felt inadequate to wrap gifts. Your comment about my statement of inadequacy was that it was my convenient way of getting out of something I didn't want to do, and we had our little spat about that. Now it is just too difficult with my repaired shoulder, and you were a bit more sympathetic to that. I used bags I had purchased at the dollar store and tissue paper. I bought a gift for everyone and for the grandkids. I included a card with cash. I felt very good being able to share gifts with a feeling that like in the past, it was a gift from both of us.

Through the whole day, I was ever conscious of your absence even though it didn't overwhelm me as some past Christmas. It all began as Jeanne and I put the presents in the car. I knew you would have had a special way to pack them so we did not do any damage. Once we got to Karen's, Garrett helped us carry them in and just threw them under the tree. I could envision you making sure that the gifts for each person were placed in a certain configuration so at the time of giving, we could get at them and distribute in the most orderly fashion. I guess the whole day began with a very real awareness that your organizational presence would be missing all day.

Karen and Bruce had the table in the kitchen area all decked out with finger foods of every kind: lots of shrimp, chips, salsas, hummus, nuts, fruit, veggies. And in the great room was a table with all the beverages. Everyone dug in as Karen carried on cooking the meal. She had a ten-pound prime rib and prepared from scratch the carrot dish you taught her and brussels sprouts. She also had mashed potatoes and made a special recipe of mac and cheese for Karlee. Bruce was a great help, but as they tried to get it all ready so it would be warm and everyone would be at the table, I mentioned to Bruce that "Mom's organizational genius is missing." And he responded, "Yes, it is!" You had the way to make sure everyone was at the table, and all the food was kept hot, and we were all ready to enjoy the meal at the right time. You always depended on me to do some of the food preparation. But setting the table with all the decorations and making sure it all worked out in a timely fashion was your gift, and again we missed it.

Nonetheless, the whole meal was delicious. Karen really outdid herself. She even made your famous Jell-O salad, and I helped her make the gravy from the prime rib drippings. It all worked out; and afterward, we had a host of desserts that Sue helped prepare, even an apple pie from the church's apple pie making event in the fall. I enjoyed a piece with vanilla ice cream, delicious but something I try to avoid for weight reasons. Before dessert, we opened gifts; and here you were again sorely missed, no little Mrs. Santa with her red hat and jingle bells sorting out the gifts so each was presented to the proper person and given the opportunity to open so all could witness and comment. Only when comments were finished did you permit the next gift to be passed on until all were opened and properly appreciated. You made the gift giving an event in itself and all were affirmed, the giver and the recipient. There were many nice gifts yesterday which all enjoyed, but the event just left something missing—you!

Since I no longer feel comfortable driving home as it gets later, we left around eight thirty. On the ride home, Richelle called. We were able to talk with her on the car phone and received info on when she was coming with Alex and Miranda on Thursday early in the morning, around 6:30 a.m. Bruce is picking them up. Jeanne and I will stop over in the morning some time. On Friday, we are going to visit Candice and bring gifts. In a text message to Karen, she agreed with that. So hopefully this will work out, and we can establish a better relationship with Candice. I will inform you about what occurs on the weekend.

Now that you are experiencing God's nearer presence, I wonder how you see our Christmas celebrations in this world in which all is not fully known. The promise according to Paul is "For now we see in a mirror dimly, but then face to face. Now I know in part; then I shall know fully, even as I have been fully known" (Corinthians 13:12).

With that, I say good night, and I love you!

Some Feelings during the Holiday Season

Dear Mae,

It's New Year's Day, and I am enjoying a respite from some of the busyness associated with having Jeanne here and spending time with the kids and grandkids. I always remember how exhausted our parents said they were after a visit from us and our kids. We, especially you, always helped as much as you could when we visited. But just being together was tiring for the older folks, and I felt that this morning. I stayed in bed until about nine fifteen. Then I didn't really fall asleep until about three fifteen, and only after taking half of a sleeping pill—so many thoughts racing through my head!

I am sure that the main reason for being so weary is that my age is catching up on me. I am sure if you had been here, both of us would be exhausted. In missing you, I sometimes forget that you would be getting older with me and would experience similar feelings. My memory will always picture you as the vibrant, vital, vivacious person you were when you were killed! It was nice having Jeanne here for a week. I am ever more aware of how much she misses you as well. You were more than a sister-in-law; you were like the sister she never had and a best friend. She mentioned you often and the various things she remembered doing with you, and often with a tear in her eye. She left on Saturday, so she had a couple opportunities to visit with the California crew and exchange gifts.

Richelle, Alex, and Miranda arrived on the twenty-seventh, two days after Christmas. Bruce picked them up from the airport, and they spent their entire stay with Bruce and Karen. We all went out to dinner a couple times and had dinner at Bruce and Karen's and exchanged gifts. One day, everyone went into New York; and according to Bruce, they walked about seven miles. They really covered the area. There were so many things they wanted to see. Even if you had been here, there would have no way we could have gone with them.

Yesterday, everyone came here to celebrate New Year's Eve. They wondered how to celebrate and were thinking of restaurants that would accommodate us, but then I suggested I make my red seafood sauce with pasta. That is what we did and is one of the reasons I am tired. If you had only been here, everything would have been so much easier. I did the cooking of the sauce; but you always helped, took care of the dishes, setting the table and all the niceties that went along with a celebration meal. Thoughts of all the artistry for decoration prompted wishes I could provide some flare, but that only contributed to the tired feelings.

I purchased all the ingredients fresh: the seafood and even the spices. That in itself was a task, just not that quick and energetic doing all of that anymore! I also feel I am losing some skill in sauce making. It just didn't taste the way I expected or remembered, sort of fumbled through preparation, not fully aware which ingredients should be added when, always feeling your help was needed, at least your companionship to make sure it would come together in the best manner possible. So often I took your presence for granted when I was cooking. This whole adjustment to living without your companionship is ever difficult, and even after working at it for over four years.

One of the greatest fears is the progressive weakness I feel. I am afraid of not being able to live on my own without some help. There were so many things you did for me which I took for granted, like rubbing lotion on my back after a shower to keep the skin soft and not itchy. I like to go into the pool here for exercise, but I do not like how my skin feels with no lotion on my back. There is no way I can even attempt putting it on with my repaired shoulder. In preparing that meal, I especially felt the need of help. That isn't like me. I tend to be quite independent, but not any longer and realize it is only going to get worse

Gratefully Richelle and Karen helped with the final preparation by getting out the dishes and setting the table. Bruce had enlarged the table by inserting the heavy wooden leaves. I have no idea what happened to the table covers we used for protection, undoubtedly got lost in our move. Everyone helped clean up afterward, and they did a great job. Karen made sure everything was very clean because she knew it would be another week before the cleaning ladies would come. Garrett also helped putting new batteries in the smoke detectors and changing the filters in the furnace, so fortunate to have their help. I just wish we lived a bit closer to each other.

Tomorrow I am going to make sure I get some good rest. I would like to go to a movie with you, or even better, a ride to Pennsylvania to look at the ski slopes we used to visit at this time of the year. This season incites so many memories. Some bring a smile and warm feelings, and others continue to provoke tears and those sad "pity pot" feelings.

Ever aware of your absence and ever grateful for your love!

It's Like Riding a Roller Coaster

⁓

Dear Mae,

"It's like riding a roller coaster!" That is how my neighbor Edith put it. Eddy, as she is known, lost her husband late summer. I mentioned her in a previous letter. I got to know them right after the purchase of the condo. Ernie and Eddy bought at about the same time, and we met quite often and engaged in conversations. He was a very affable man, and we discovered we had a connection, both lived in Clifton. He and Eddy lived there for many years, so we often conversed about familiar places and people.

When we first met, he appeared healthy and eager to start a new experience in condo living. The first summer, we often got together at the pool and enjoyed kibitzing. One day, he injured his foot tripping on something, not altogether sure what or how. Anyway, it resulted in an infection and grew to be rather serious since he was diabetic. In the course of recovery, he spent some time in rehab and recovered enough to return home, but it seemed like he never gained the strength and vitality he had previously. The injury to his foot never healed completely and appeared to produce or reveal other health issues. Over time, it went from bad to worse. He was hospitalized on various occasions. All efforts to recover fully seemed futile. Suddenly one morning, he died. The family knew he was not improving but were not prepared for his sudden passing. Many people in the building were touched because he had become an enjoyable friend.

Since then, Eddy has been trying hard to adjust. On occasion we talked, and I purchased a copy of *Option B* for her. In turn, she wanted to show appreciation and purchased a doorbell for my condo. When we meet each other, we stop and talk, and the other day her comment about riding a roller coaster got to me. It often describes my feelings. One day, I awake and, at the moment of awareness, feel the vibes of a good day to follow, and a good feeling day follows. I have plenty of energy for the tasks to accomplish and energy left over to discover new and interesting activity. Other days, even before I feel awake, I want to stay in bed, feel very little challenge to confront the day's duties. I don't want to go out and meet people or even make contact on Facebook or the phone.

Henry Nouwen describes these feelings this morning in a piece on the website that lists various sayings from his numerous writings. "A little criticism makes me angry, and a little rejection makes me depressed. A little praise raises my spirits, and a little success excites me. *It takes very little to raise me up or thrust me down.* Often, I am like a small boat on the ocean, completely at the mercy of its waves. All the time and energy I spend in keeping some kind of balance and preventing myself from being tipped over and drowning" (not sure of date published, sent out as e-mail by Henry Nouwen Society).

I get upset because of these feelings! I am aware it does not help build an attitude that moves me to be a people helper, but then it is not good to deny these feelings either, just need to find a way to get out of them and get back on top of the roller coaster. I definitely need to be more patient, and something or someone will come along to help like just happened. The phone rang, and it was Peter Ferguson wishing me a happy New Year. He had lunch with Don Small, and both had thought of me he said. That would be natural since both have lost their wives since you died, and both of their wives were your friends. We had attended a lot of happy functions as couples, and Don and I played golf together.

Perhaps one of the reasons my frequent being on the downside of the roller coaster is that I am getting older. I know I mention this often, but there have been more times when I don't feel the greatest. That is a fact! This roller coaster affects where the moods change more often and are more deeply felt seems to be due to being older, weaker, and vulnerable. Ever since the stem cell transplant, I have noticed periods when the body hurts quite a bit; and with your passing, that has only increased. I often wonder how you would be experiencing life now that you would be eighty-one. You went through some difficult health issues in our marriage and survived them all, but with a lot of discomfort. You always seemed to manage in a way that brought out the best in your person. Other people never suffered because you did. I feel that is not always the way it is with me.

I'm counting on making 2019 a year in which I work harder on keeping a positive attitude even in the throes of my loneliness.

Love ya, hon!

Christmas with Candice

Hi, honey.

It has been a while since the last letter. So many things have happened I have been reading and thinking about so much I don't know where to begin this letter. I have named it Christmas with Candice, so I will begin there. We—that is, Karen, Richelle, Jeanne, Karlee, Alex, and Miranda—all visited Candice on December 28, three days after Christmas and the day after the West Coast family members arrived.

It was with a lot of anxiety for all of us. How would she greet us? Karen had arranged the visit communicating with her on Skype. When Jeanne and I arrived, the others were already present with Candice in the living room. Candice looked very unhealthy, thin, ashen, and weak. She was pleasant; and before we could present our gifts, she had a gift for each of us, even Alex, Karlee, and Miranda. She had purchased cards and addressed one to each with a cash gift of twenty-five dollars. It was obvious that as always before at Christmas, she was pleased and proud to be able to offer these gifts. She smiled and handed out each with care and apparent pleasure. It was the happiest I have seen her since last Christmas.

Karen gave her a neat tee shirt and Jeanne a cash gift. My gift had been a check sent before Christmas and also some chocolates. She graciously acknowledged all the gifts. We stayed for almost an hour and shared some of the things we were doing, and she seemed to be quite interested. When we invited her to do some things with us over the next couple days while Richelle and her children were with us, she politely refused as she has regularly done when invited to join. When we were there almost an hour, it became obvious she was getting tired. So we decided it best to leave, and she seemed relieved to be able to bid us farewell. She didn't want any hugs or kisses. She just waved and wished everyone well, thanking us for the gifts.

It is very difficult to describe, let alone capture my feelings. For a brief moment, it felt like a dead person had come back to life. As we mentioned past experiences and people, she commented on them as well and remembered the persons seemingly better than I did. For a moment, it was like the Candice of the past who always had such a good memory. It appeared that in some things, she still has it, but her illness presents such a mystery. Why all the hostility at times, and why this brief interlude in which she was showing us her love? For a couple minutes, I had a flashback to her energy, liveliness, and vivacity. And then it was like a shade was drawn, and all was dark again. Leaving without a hug or even an endearing word was very difficult. Tears filled my eyes as I slowly went down the stairs in front of the house. It was depressing and despairing.

As we left, we agreed to meet for dinner at a diner in Little Falls. It would be halfway between Karen's, where Richelle and family were staying, and my place in Wharton where Jeanne was staying with me. All of us felt grateful that Candice welcomed us and even more so that she would gift us as she did. We were conflicted about her cash gifts. Here she is on disability, and she gives us cash of which we have more than enough. We should be doing the giving, not her. But no, it is a sign that she is still alive, and the vibrant spirit that she always had cannot be darkened by her disease. She is still able to find a way to make life a joy for someone else. The people in the house where she lives would always mention that she was most helpful to them. Although it ever remains a mystery, she is able to live with a sense of meaning, and I am perplexed because I am no longer recognized as her father. Sometimes we simply have to accept life without trying to understand.

Well, the other things I wanted to write will have to wait. There is always another day, and it never gets easier dealing with it and not being able to get your feedback.

I can't stop hurting because I loved you so much, and of course, still do even if all I have now is a memory and pictures.

Death Strikes

Dear Mae,

It has been a depressing couple of weeks. A number of our friends have died. I guess this is the age when more and more of them are going to join you in the great mystery of God's nearer presence. A couple of weeks ago, Wes Kort called informing me that both Karl de Jonge and Dick Houskamp were in hospice care. Fortunately, I have been able to talk with both. Karl told me that he was pain-free and being well cared for by the hospice associated with the Holland Home in Grand Rapids. We shared some great memories, especially of the trip we took from Calvin to New Jersey back in the fifties, before you and I met. It was one of those good buddies' trips. We met Jim Kok at Westminster Seminary and Arnie Rottman at a bar in Clifton, on Broad Street. Who thought at that time that I would one day live there as a pastor of a nearby church? Karl died a couple of days following our conversation. Joan called to inform me. We enjoyed a lengthy memory-filled conversation.

Joan gave me Dick and Alyce's cell phone number, and I called. They were checking into the hospice unit at the time, so I told them I would call back the next day, which I did. Dick was very weak, and we only were able to talk a few minutes. His pain was severe. I don't exactly remember where his cancer began, but it has metastasized to the bones and was very painful. Karl had hospice at home, but because of Dick's condition, he had to be in a unit where they could constantly manage his pain. It must have been very severe because he said, "I am ready to die, and I hope it is quick because the pain is unbearable." He died a few days later. His funeral was held in Calvin Chapel while they were experiencing heavy snow. Rusty wanted to attend, but as close as they live to Calvin, he didn't risk going.

Another of our friends, Cal Heerschap, died on Friday. I don't think I have written to you about Cal. Sometime last summer, he posted on Facebook that he was in the hospital. I decided to visit and found him to be confused about his condition. He didn't know what caused it, but it had progressed to a point where he could hardly walk. He was weak, tired, and losing weight. He remained in the hospital for almost two weeks. It was a couple of weeks after release that he went back again, same symptoms! This kind of situation continued until about four weeks ago when he was hospitalized for the last time and was informed he was going to die. He called me before anyone else and didn't know how to tell me about it. He said a doctor had just said, "You know you are going to die!" Naturally, Cal was devastated. We talked quite a while and often since. I also visited him. I tried to help him build some hope, and I think I did, but also became aware he had chosen to live in denial of what was taking place. His liver had shut down, and they had to do repeated procedures to remove body fluid. This past, Friday he died. Daughter Gwen, who lives in Connecticut, called and requested that I conduct services on Saturday at Allwood Funeral Home in Clifton.

There are a number of reasons I share this with you. First of all, because at one time, all these people were very close friends; and when I think of them, I think of us together as their friends. I believe Karl's wife Joan studied organ with you at Calvin, and Karl and I kept in touch through the years. We met a couple times on our trips to Florida, and once we met, it was like we had never been apart. I picked up where we had been years before. Dick was the buddy who coaxed me to ask you for our first date, and we had that date when we doubled with him and Alyce and went bowling on a Saturday night. I had mentioned to him that I thought you were really attractive. Because you, he, and Alyce all sang in the choir, he knew you would welcome a date and urged me to ask. So that is where we began. It was that date that gave me the feeling you were the one. I don't think you felt that way at the time, but it turned out to be wonderfully true. Our friendship with Dick and Alice, continued and I was asked to perform their wedding ceremony, which took place in Chicago. In recent years, we lost touch.

Cal and Nancy were some of the good friends we made while living in Clifton. The friendship with Cal grew after the death of Nancy. That was most difficult for him, and who knew that the thoughts I shared to help him through those crisis days would have to be remembered a decade and half later to help me get through the crisis of losing you? In preparing for what to say at Cal's memorial service, I was brought back to many of the feelings I repeatedly experienced following your loss, and I am sure, will continue to feel.

Yesterday, I had breakfast with Frank Weisse. He told me that he looks forward to us getting together because it enables him to gain the strength needed to go on. He also told me about a couple of people who also lost loved ones and recently have had the experience of these dead family members reappearing with them. He wanted to know what I thought of that. These experiences were revealed to him as being very real and vivid, and it has caused him to be a bit apprehensive, wondering if his wife Ann may reappear some day. He worries how he may react. I never really worried about you reappearing; but as I think I have already told you, the day after your funeral, a cardinal appeared in the tree above our driveway as I went out to retrieve the morning paper. The bird made a lot of noise, and I felt you were there, calling to me. It not only made me feel you were okay but also that you would never fully leave me.

Since then, I haven't had any specific bird visits, but I consistently get the feeling that you are somewhere near. At times, I feel I see you for a second, and then you are gone. I don't really know what to make of it other than you are ever looking after me. Anyway, that is my hope.

I will get back to this letter after Cal's funeral. I have put a good deal of time into preparation. Ironically, I received a call from Scanlan's as I was writing the funeral message asking if I would be willing to do a funeral for a man who was a member at Pompton Plains Church while I was the pastor. I remember him and his wife. I have seen them recently at church but don't want to do any funerals unless it's a close friend like Cal. It is not the work so much as not feeling sure of myself when under stress. I have had a few almost-dizzy moments lately and think it could be related to minor stress I feel from taking on responsibilities like doing a funeral. I will share with you how I get through this one with Cal. I don't think there will be a large turnout, and we are not going to a burial site.

Back after the funeral! I was wrong. There was a big crowd. Cal touched many lives. They had to put in extra chairs, and even then, people had to stand. I met many old Clifton acquaintances. First people to greet me as I walked in was Jay Baker, for whose wife I did a funeral service some years ago, and Joey Firsh, who forty years ago, was a little kid down the street. There were others—Karen Davoui, Janice Hoeke, who remembered you walking out of choir in the middle of worship to turn on the oven for the roast for our Sunday dinner. You had put the roast in the oven before you left but never turned on the oven, so much like you, always having too many things to do just before you had to be some place. Janice was always very fond of you.

Overall, it was a better experience than anticipated. I do feel I spoke to the pain and hurts felt by family and friends, and I didn't come away overly tired. I did not go to the repast however. I knew it would get late, and I would have to drive home in the dark. Mike Porter, the funeral director, said to me, "You haven't lost it. You still know how to preach." I have heard that quite often since you died. I sort of think it is one of those kinds of things people say to old preachers, affirming them. Enough for now!

All my love.

Loneliness

Good morning, honey!

It is a rather nice morning for the first week in February. In fact, this week, we had temperatures as high as 60°, and they are predicting the 60s for tomorrow. It's a nice day to take a walk; however, walking in this community is not easy. There are too many hills, and I find it is increasingly more difficult catching my breath walking up hills.

I would like to talk with you this morning about loneliness. I've looked through the letters previously written, and although my feeling of loneliness is mentioned often, I haven't concentrated on it in a single letter. Just want to share a couple thoughts. This morning, I read a devotional taken from the writings of Henry Nouwen. His piece began:

> Whenever you feel lonely, you must try to find the source of this feeling. You are inclined either to run away from your loneliness or to dwell in it. When you run away from it, your loneliness does not really diminish; you simply force it out of your mind temporarily. When you start dwelling in it, your feelings only become stronger, and you slip into depression.

In another piece, he added this:

> To live a spiritual life we must first find the
> courage to enter into the desert of our loneliness
> and to change it by gentle and persistent efforts
> into a garden of solitude.

When I try to reflect on my loneliness, it seems to be closely tied in with events that create sadness. I feel most lonely when something happens that hurts and causes emotional pain and there is no one to share it who fully understands the depth of the sadness. A very apt example happened yesterday. I was walking in the mall hoping to find a present for Bruce's birthday when my phone rang. It was somebody from Newbridge Services. He wanted to know if I was the father of Candice Rienstra. When I said yes, he responded saying that a procedure was being planned for her at St. Claire's Hospital the next day and that someone would be contacting me from the hospital staff. He said to be ready for a phone call.

It immediately hit me in the pit of the stomach. Could this be the end for her? I recalled the last time I saw her and how emaciated and weak she appeared. She had not been eating and was continuing to have problems swallowing. I thought that this was the first time I have ever been contacted by health-care people about her condition. It must be very serious; otherwise, they wouldn't break the HIPAA rules. I promptly found a chair to sit down in the food court and began to cry, feeling all alone in the midst of a throng of people all around. Up to that point in the day, I had been feeling good. I have gotten beyond that point in grieving where I feel lonely most of the time. Now it comes only when things like this occur. It is at such a moment I want to be with you, talk with you. No one else can fill that void.

How should I respond to this? It has been almost forty years that we have dealt with the sad condition of Candice's illness, and we always faced times of crisis together. We only made the big decisions relating to her after we talked together, prayed together, and then made moves, some of them quite risky. Now here I was all alone, allowing my mind to think about what the problem might be, and no one to cool down my imagination with the caution not to let my fears get the best of me.

It wasn't long, and a doctor called. He was slightly reassuring. He said that they needed to do an endoscopy to see if there was anything further down in the esophagus that was impeding the passage of food and medications. He explained that in talking with her, she agreed to the procedure. But because her psychiatrist didn't think she was mentally competent to make decisions for herself, they needed to find a guardian, and the only name they had was mine. This decision was also related to the fact that she has not been willing to take her medications and has been refusing them. He said they were aware she didn't want any of her family to know but felt that her condition was such that for her well-being, she had to be overruled. Of course, I agreed knowing that such a procedure was not life-threatening and could possibly help alleviate the problem she has been living with for some time.

Because of what transpired, I have interrupted this letter. What has happened has heightened my aloneness. Immediately following the procedure, the doctor called and told me that Candice had a very small opening at the top of the esophagus for food to pass, and they had stretched it. He also said she had a pyloric ulcer at the stomach entrance and wanted to examine it in a couple weeks. He told me she would remain in the hospital over the weekend. Unfortunately, that was not true.

They shipped her out of the hospital to a rehab facility, Care One in Parsippany, that very night. I discovered this Saturday morning and immediately went to see her. I was very concerned about how she would respond since she never wanted me to have anything to do with her health care, especially since your death. All my fears were for naught because I found her unable to respond. She slowly opened her eyes for a moment and then went right back to sleep. Realizing that she often doesn't wake until later in the afternoon, I sat with her for a while and then left. I didn't talk with any staff people because it seemed everyone was busy, and I assumed I would come back to discover more with Karen the next day. I also received a call from a therapist who asked me a number of questions, which made me think they were putting together a plan for rehabbing her, getting her back to receiving nutrition and gaining physical strength.

After church Sunday morning, Karen and I visited Care One. We found Candice looking terrible. She was lying in bed, unable to respond to us. Karen called out her name, touched her, tried a number of things to arouse her, but no luck. We immediately went to the desk on the unit, talked to who was obviously in charge at that time and also the nurse assigned to Candice. To our shock, we discovered she had taken in no food or water since her arrival on Friday night. Karen was furious and demanded that they immediately hook her up to an IV. They couldn't because they didn't have doctor's orders. In no uncertain tone, we told them to *get* doctor's orders. They realized we were livid. And within fifteen minutes, doctor's orders were obtained, and she was hooked up to at least hydration. They told us they couldn't do more because it was the weekend, and they had to wait until Monday morning for the staff to get busy with her. We remained for a while simply watching Candice lie there; and as it seemed, she was perking up a bit, but still too weak to communicate with us. We made plans for a visit the next day and contacted the people at Newbridge Services home in Boonton (South Terrace Manor) where Candice was living.

Going home from the care center, I felt terribly lonely. It was at those crisis moments we meant so much to each other. We had gone through so many in our life with both daughters Candice and Karen. I recalled the first time a psychiatrist had indicated that the illness discovered with Candice was probably something for which there was no cure, just medication to hopefully keep it in control. I talked with him on my study phone at church and returned home immediately to talk with you about how we would manage such a journey. That only led to more and more episodes in which we leaned on each other to get through the crisis. I remember the time we didn't know where she was and searched out the various homeless shelters only to be told they wouldn't tell us even if they knew where she was.

So many tough times! While making my bed this morning, I just said, "God, I have had enough, four bouts with cancer, stem cell replacement, shoulder surgery, loss of you, and now this with Candice! Enough! And I could add much more." I felt so lonely and didn't want to get going but realized in my thinking, as Nouwen said, that loneliness has to develop into solitude that enables one to face the next time with greater strength. I know I have grown through all this since your death; I've become more focused on most things (sometimes I think too focused). I lose awareness of how to have fun. I got to get back into that. I made up my mind that I am going to accept more offers from neighbors to do things together. I have done a lot of refusing social involvement, choosing to be with myself, which doesn't bring genuine solitude.

I will share more of this Candice episode as it develops. As a friend said to me last night, "Mae is watching over you. She won't let this get the best of you." Hopefully that is true!

Love you so much.

More on Candice

Good Presidents' Day, hon! A lot has transpired in the past couple days, and I haven't found time to write. The last was about our time in Care One with Candice last Sunday. On Monday, I stopped at South Terrace Manor to get some information about how they determined to send her to St. Claire's since she had previously been treated by doctors at Chilton.

Their story was that the ambulance service would only take her to St. Claire's, and they were very concerned she should get to a hospital as soon as possible. She was getting so weak, refusing to eat, and not taking her meds. It was evidently at St. Claire's that a psychiatrist decided she needed an advocate, as she was too mentally ill to make medical decisions for herself.

After visiting with and gathering more information from the staff, I met Karen at Care One. The staff there told us that they had plans to rehabilitate Candice, get her to eat, and bring her strength back. Karen was not happy about that. She wanted her moved immediately. I called the Chilton doctors and inquired about having Candice sent there. And they were open, but also said that maybe the rehab which might be done at Care One could work, but they hadn't seen her. So to sum it up, we left her there that Monday and were not able to get back to see her on Tuesday because of stormy weather. When we did get back on Wednesday, her condition was unchanged from Monday, if not a bit worse. She seemed weaker and was unable to communicate. She did seem to know we were there; and we face-timed with Richelle, showed it to Candice, and she was able to give a little wave. However, we were very unsatisfied with what was taking place. We met with a physician's assistant who admitted she needed more acute care, and we had her transported to Chilton on Wednesday late afternoon.

Karen and I arrived shortly after Candice and met with the attending doctor and nurses. They did the appropriate tests and later that evening, brought her to a room on the fourth floor. It was a large single room next to the nurse's station where they could easily watch her. During the ten days she was there, the staff did everything they knew to get her out of the catatonic stage she experienced. There were CAT scans and a test to measure brain waves. Nothing produced anything conclusive, and we finally came to the conclusion to send her for hospice care. This was very difficult because the nourishment they gave her through a nasal-gastric tube had improved her overall health. Her skin and eyes looked better even though her ability to communicate did not improve. She remained in a mostly catatonic condition. After watching her in that condition for five days, we decided this was not the way she would want to live, nor was it the way the girls and I would want to live, and we believed the same would be true for you.

We were given a couple of hospice options, and the hospital staff worked at reaching out to these facilities. The one we chose was Vitas at St. Joseph's Hospital in Wayne. It is right next to the old Wayne Hospital. She has been transferred there from the hospital and is receiving excellent care. There is a fine staff of nurses and social workers, and even a chaplain. They all appear to be well trained and prepared for their task. The question that haunts me is, how come she became like this? What happened following that endoscopy that has produced this semi-conscious state? Since she went into the hospital lucid and even a bit cantankerous, what caused her to lose her sense of what is going on and how to communicate? Finding an answer to that question is driving me right now. I have talked at length with John (my physician brother) who is convinced that there was a screwup someplace along the line of performing the procedure.

I have contacted the hospital and asked for an answer, but the person who is the patient's advocate has not gotten back to me even though she said she would do so two days ago. This makes me even more disturbed. I sure wish we could talk together about this. You always had such wise counsel when it came to dealing with these situations. I am going to contact a couple friends in the corporate world for advice. John is pushing me to be confrontative and let them know we are going to get a lawyer. I have been thinking about it all day, hoping they would contact me with some reasonable information. I'm not sure of my next move. For now, I am going to get some rest. It is bedtime!

Love ya.

Candice and Hospice Care

Dear Mae,

It's a sunny Monday morning in March after a weekend of storms. For New Jersey, we had quite a bit of snow, again not as much as you would like to see. You were always disappointed with New Jersey snow and often wished we could just have one of those big Michigan snows you enjoyed while in college. Well, yesterday was big enough for me. It started about 4:00 p.m. and continued through the night, and this morning, the view from my bedroom window was spectacular. Standing in the kitchen and looking at the windows in the living room, it appeared like a giant ski slope. What I could not see from that perspective with my failing vision is that it was snow on tree limbs which, from where I stood, looked like a huge mountain with a multitude of ski trails.

All that beauty has not made my day. The reason? I'm sick, an upper respiratory infection of some kind. I don't know where I contracted the bug, but think it is as bad as I have experienced since you left. I lay in bed last night, having a tough time breathing and remembering how you put Vicks on the bottom of my feet, claiming that it would be helpful in enabling breathing. I really needed that therapy last night. I only slept in stages, far apart. I couldn't stop coughing, not sure I have a thermometer to check for a fever. This all comes at a time when I really want to be at the hospice unit to be with Candice.

I did go to see her yesterday, which I probably shouldn't have. I was feeling pretty good, but I think the effort put into making a visit was not the best for my condition. She was more alert than any time since her endoscopy. She was even able to breath out a soft "yeah" to some of the questions we asked. Karen was also there. Although the question remains why she cannot communicate, it seems more likely, after conversations with the hospice staff, it could be due to the weakness she developed by refusing to eat and take her meds. It almost seems that she chose not to eat. We note how she refuses food from the hospice staff even when it appears she could swallow. They are beginning to give her pureed food and more liquid, and she seems to be gaining some strength but is very deliberate in choosing what and how much she will eat. Undoubtedly, we need to be patient to discover what may develop with the nutrition she is getting. They are contemplating sending her to another facility. Her present unit is designed more for close to end-of-life care. She doesn't need that right now. She needs the care that will determine if she can snap back to normality.

For two reasons I don't think I will visit her today. One is the weather. The roads still need considerable cleaning. I also do not want to subject Candice to whatever bug is affecting me.

As I said in the last writing, I did not visit Candice for a couple days. The main reason was my present battle with this virus. I don't want to share it and especially want to get enough rest to eliminate it. However, yesterday I had to do some things I've been postponing. I shopped for some household necessities and followed up on getting medical records. The day began as a disaster! My toilet blocked up and created a mess. Since the cleaning ladies were due in, I wanted to get it unblocked before they came so they could clean up whatever mess it might make.

I borrowed a plunger from a neighbor, and using it made an even greater mess. I finally had to contact a repair man I used previously who came and immediately resolved the issue, but it all took a toll emotionally. I hadn't eaten any breakfast, still felt the effects of the virus, and wanted to crawl back in bed. I so missed you! I felt as lonely as I have, helpless, not sure of what would be the next move. I did not want to burden Karen. She has enough going on and has been so helpful. I don't know what I would do without her.

The cleaning ladies arrived, and I went for breakfast and then to the hospital for the medical records only to discover that I need some papers to authenticate me as the power of attorney, or the advocate for Candice. Since I have signed papers at every place she has been in the last month, I was never given a copy to carry with me, so no records. But it would not have helped me get them anyway. I need to be the official guardian since she has never changed her decision that no one could be given that information without her consent. I could sign for a medical procedure, but not get the results. Strange! From there, I went to the bank and the commissary. As I was returning to the garage in our building, Karen called. Since the phone doesn't work there, I carried all the things up to the condo and called her back.

Karen informed me that the hospice people were ready to move Candice to another unit, and we should look at where they might take her to see if we would be pleased with the place and people. The first place we visited was Regency Gardens on Hamburg Turnpike, not far from her present facility. It looked good to us, but not nearly as nice as where she was. We met the director, we were given a tour, and after some thought and conversation between us and staff, decided it would be a satisfactory place for her. Although it is basically a nursing home, it allows the hospice team to work there with patients who are living longer than anticipated. That very evening, they moved Candice. But it was late, and we determined that we would stop by the next morning to visit. I leave this letter and continue with what happened from there in a new letter.

Love and miss you so much at this time!

"Left to right, Candice, Richelle and Karen. The sisters did their best to care for Candice during her final days. Richelle came from California."

Candice's Final Days

My dearest Mae,

This has to be one of the toughest letters I've written. Candice died at 4:30 a.m. on March 19, 2019. A hospice nurse woke me with the news at four forty-five. The moment the phone rang, I knew. I called Karen, and we both cried. Since Richelle was with me, she got up and helped make our next moves. I hadn't mentioned that Richelle came at the end of last week. It had been a tough week from the time Candice had been transferred to Regency Gardens until that phone call. I really don't have any complaints on how she was treated there, but it just didn't have the ambiance, attractiveness, and attention of the first place she stayed. Her room was a double, whereas she had a large single previously, one in which we could visit anytime and stay as long as we wished.

Because this place was basically a nursing home, it had all the features of the same. There were carts with dirty linens just outside her door, and the odor was ever-present. There were people in various stages of physical repair walking back and forth since it also provided rehab for elderly and injured persons. Since all the staff was not hospice, treatment was restricted. Hospice staff people showed up regularly, but they were not there 24/7.

I told the staff that they should contact Scanlan's Funeral Home and they would pick up the body. It is kind of difficult to remember the sequence of things that happened after that. I know I contacted Pastor Kathleen and set up an appointment with the funeral home staff. Since Candice had no clothes or personal belongings with her, we did not have to pick up after her. If I can recall correctly, I think the three of us spent the day having a meeting with the funeral home staff and ate lunch with Kathleen. It was one of those days that I never want to repeat.

It is so difficult for me to accept her death. She was our firstborn, and we loved her immensely. She was so vital, so alive, so ready to challenge what we knew about being parents. She brought so much joy to our early life together. I remember one night lying in bed with her, reading stories, helping her get to sleep, and thinking how would I ever be able to deal with losing her. Now I know, and even though it is years later, it feels like it is even more difficult than when I lost you. I think it is because we always figured we would lose each other someday, but we seldom thought about losing a child, regardless of how old we became. It could also be that since we lost the person who she was when she became mentally ill, we always had the hope that some medication, some method of therapy, would correct the situation and restore her to being the vital, vigorous person she was prior to her hearing those voices. Your loss hit me hard, but it seems that I dealt with it more effectively than I am dealing with the loss of Candice. It seems like every time someone talks with me about her, asks questions, or wants to know something about her history, my eyes begin to water. I try to turn off the faucet, but sometimes I can't, and the tears flow. But then I must be forgetting those first weeks without you. I am sure I was the same with my emotions.

Enough of this for now. I will get back to you soon and tell you about the wonderful celebration of her life we planned and enjoyed. The very sad part of it was that you were not there to tell us of how you enjoyed being her mother in those early years.

Love ya, hon.

The Celebration of Life

Hi, hon.

It has been a while since the last letter. I have been so busy catching up on stuff I put writing aside because of involvement with Candice. It was tax time, and I had to complete my returns with TurboTax. In the process, my computer began running really slow, so slow I took it to the Apple Store to get it checked out. After running a test, the technician informed me that it was ten years old, and the processor was having a difficult time keeping up with all the updates. He told me that it would still run, although slowly, and I should think of a new unit. I agreed but said I needed to wait until after the taxes were finished because I didn't want to risk losing all that I had already finished, which could happen if I switched to a new machine. I suppose there was a way to avoid that, but I didn't want to take the risk. As I picked up the computer and began to leave, I dropped it on the floor. Members of the working staff picked it up and tested it to see if it would still run. It did, but the screen was scratched and broken on the top right corner.

It turned out to be a fortunate drop. I was informed that since the accident happened in the Apple Store, I could get a new computer for 25 percent off. I have taken advantage of the offer and now have a new computer, a twenty-seven-inch iMac and am writing this letter on it. I used the old one to finish my taxes and then brought it in to get this one. I'm happy I used the old one for the taxes because the data will not show on this new one. I'm not going to do much research on that right now because I was able to file and pay and will work on how I can retrieve that info on this machine in a few weeks, no hurry.

Well, about the funeral service for Candice, it was truly a tribute to her and her battle with mental illness. We had a trumpeter, and he was very good, brought tears. John and Amy sang. Karen spoke. I will add her words as an appendage to these letters when published. Richelle spoke and read a poem Jane Style had written about Candice and her trumpet being transferred to a new dimension. I spoke about our struggle with her illness and our determination to use her illness to help others fight mental illness. Kathleen had a very uplifting message in which she used a Greek word for the splitting of the heavens at Jesus's baptism, which is a root for the word *schizoid*. She also talked about how she saw you waiting for Candice on the other side of the veil of separation. So I hope what she saw is what is!

Jane Okma, who had a friendship with Candice that began at Montclair State during the time they were both students there, spoke. She creatively shared how Candice was such a help to her and how much she appreciated Candice's friendship. Carolyn Dean, a staff member at South Terrace Manor, also spoke about Candice's contribution to the family of people living there. She told how Candice would add to the times of celebration with her keyboard music and trumpet and how she was always so willing to help everyone. She made it apparent that mentally ill people could make significant contributions to the community and that Candice had done that.

The service was livestreamed, and our brother-in-law Jim Meyer put it on YouTube. I have watched it twice since, and it has been an inspiration each time. I cry through it and realize those tears are good for me. All the stress of what took place in the last weeks of her life has been heavy. Although Richelle and Karen have been a great source of companionship, there is no presence like yours to give the strength I wanted, and it wasn't to be. In gratitude for all the support I have received, I am buying two tables at the annual Newbridge Gala scheduled next month and inviting a number of those who were part of the service to be guests. I'm also inviting members of the staff at South Terrace Manor to join with us. In all, I am hopeful there will be twenty of us at two tables. This is a way to thank Newbridge for the care of Candice and some people who supported our family during this time of grieving. I wish you could be with us!

Love ya.

Easter and Karen's Birthday

Hi, hon.

You were especially missed this weekend. Everything came together at the same time: Good Friday, Passover, Easter, and Karen's Birthday. I didn't pay any attention to the first two but enjoyed the last two. Easter was very nice. I went to church in Pompton Plains with Karen, Bruce, Garrett, and Karlee. It was a nice service with a brass group, and the choir was expanded by a number of singers John Hellyer enlisted. All sounded very good. Church was not as crowded as in our day. People just are not attending church like they did in the past, too many other opportunities and too much money to enjoy them.

There is a worship team that works on creative art in worship, and they used flowers and large white ribbons to enhance the sanctuary to be very festive in appearance. All the decorations were attractive and symbolic of new life. We bought some flowers in memory of both you and Candice. Kathleen did a good job with her sermon. Listening, I realized again just how difficult it is to preach on Easter, especially after a holy week of services and responsibilities and all the expectations people have of an Easter message. I remember how through the years, I had some great sermons, so I thought; and then there were those I struggled through in writing and presentation. I never felt I had a real bad one because of the extraordinary subject matter for the day, but I didn't feel the best about some of them.

After church, we went to Karen's, and they did their preparation of the food they were taking to Korky and Sue's where we had dinner. We also took a family picture. We wanted to do it under the tree at the manse as we had through the years, but Josh wasn't with us. Dinner was good: ham, potatoes, carrots as you made them, beans, and asparagus. I bought a chocolate cake at Costco, but I didn't have any. After we ate, Sue took us to view the new addition to the Holland Home. When we were done with that, I left for home. I have been very tired the last week, and I just wanted to get back to the condo.

This morning, I called Karen to wish her happy birthday and also made a date for lunch with her, Bruce, and whoever wanted to come. We went to the Blue Moon, that Mexican restaurant near the department store we often shopped at in the mall in Wyckoff. Only Garrett and Bruce came along. We had a nice time, and all had delicious salads. I gave Karen a gift certificate to Massage Envy in Wayne. In addition to massages, they have a lot of body ointments and creams she likes.

As to my tired feelings. I went to the doctor last week, feeling good and all my marks were good. However, I mentioned that my legs ache when I walk, and I wondered about it. She suggested I get off my statin for ten days to see if that would help, and if it did, she would put me on another that would act differently. Perhaps the one I was on was part of the problem. Remember how you wished I didn't take them? You were not high on the usefulness of statins from what you read. Well, after two days, I began to feel very tired. I am not sure if that is the cause or if an extra-long workout in the pool on Saturday might be the culprit. I will give it a couple more days, and if I don't feel better, I will call her and talk about getting back on the statin I was taking. Now I feel I should not have complained to her and just accepted the aching legs as part of aging, which I think it is. Anyway, I'm suffering from it. I will talk by letter with you next time about how it goes. I wish I could just do that in person tonight! Now to bed with the hope that sleep will be better than the last couple nights!

All my love.

Newbridge Gala

Good morning, hon! I didn't sleep real well last night. I am finding that if I have a high energy evening, my sleep is readily interrupted. That happened last night since I attended the annual Newbridge Services Gala. It was held at The Legacy Castle on Route 23 just south of Alexander Avenue in Pompton Plains. It's new since you left, very large and glitzy, not at all in keeping with the community culture of Pompton Plains. For the last couple years, Newbridge has used the place for its annual gala. I have been told it was built to serve weddings of as much as a thousand people.

As I mentioned previously, this year, I purchased two tables for ten people each. Since there was money left from the special-needs trust created for Candice, I decided to use part of it to thank people who supported us through her illness, especially those who cared for her at South Terrace Manor. We all had a very nice evening, a tasty dinner, and an opportunity to reconnect with people from the community who were part of our past.

One of the experiences was a conversation I had with a social worker who was on the staff at South Terrace Manor. She evidently spent considerable time talking with Candice. She told me that she talked extensively with Candice following your death, realizing she needed some grief support. She related that Candice became very agitated and angry when she tried to discuss how Candice was dealing with your death. She indicated that it never got better, that she didn't want to discuss your death at all. This surprised me. I knew she had not gone through any kind of grieving therapy, but I was not sure how that affected her. Now I realize it was a bigger stage in her life than all of us were aware. I think we should have become more conscious of that from very soon after your funeral. Maybe we should have taken part of the day following just to be with her and concentrate on the needs that she developed because of your loss. It became quite obvious to me that she was fearful about a number of things, particularly who would care for her money needs, since you were gone. I am sure this was related to her knowledge that you took care of other needs, like helping her choose clothes and other necessities. She really didn't want me involved in some of those things. I remember that when I tried to assure her that all would be okay because I would take care of it, she was not very pleased. I think part of her refusal to recognize me as her father recently was a deliberate act and prompted by the fact that I was taking over doing things for her she wanted you to do.

It was shortly after your funeral that her attitude toward me changed. Although she was quite guarded in what she wanted to share with us, her willingness to communicate with me became very guarded. Every time I made contact with her, the first response was "What do you want?" or "What are you doing here?" It was as if she was annoyed by the fact that I was coming to visit her. She didn't like it when I tried to call her either. As time passed, this break in communication even became more broken. She eventually didn't want anything to do with me and even cut down on her willingness to communicate with Karen. The story I shared with you about me trying to celebrate her last birthday typifies how severe her unwillingness to have me around became. I now understand her extreme anger was definitely part of a grieving process through which she was not able to navigate.

It was a revelation for me to hear what the social worker shared. I am perturbed with myself for not recognizing that earlier and trying to find ways in which I could deal with her anger and help her work through it. I might have gone to a counselor to discuss the matter and perhaps discovered means to use to improve the situation. Since I didn't do that, I went to bed last night and let those thoughts bounce around my mind which kept me from sleep. One thought that came was that she may have chosen not to eat as an act of suicide so she could again be with you. Sounds strange, but I had that thought. Others have also shared with me that possibility.

Again, this is one of those times when having lost you creates a huge void. I wish we could have talked about this! I did talk about it with a friend who is very understanding, but nothing can serve my needs like a conversation with you and the awareness of our long-term relationship in which we struggled so mightily with how best to relate to Candice. Nonetheless, it is good to have this conversation by means of this letter.

Perhaps more about this sometime later. For now, although you are physically absent, my love for who you are is as strong as ever.

Baseball and Lew Schafer

Good morning, joy of my life.

As I begin this new day, I am thinking about how I managed living without you. It is prompted by a call to Lew Schafer. I had just talked with him and Linda on Sunday as they thanked me for uniting them in a marriage ceremony twenty-eight years previously. They were celebrating on the weekend and were quite jovial. On Tuesday morning, I found out that Linda had a massive heart attack on Sunday evening and never recovered. She died less than forty-eight hours later. As soon as I found out (because of social media we find these things out almost instantaneously), I called Lew, and he had just returned from the hospital where she died. I shed some tears with him as he described the last hours of her life and his trauma. Listening, I couldn't help feeling blessed not having to suffer such an experience prior to your sudden death. It had to be excruciating for him to hear the various reports from the medical team working to keep her alive. It seemed to me that it was also like riding a roller coaster. There was hope, then sheer fear, and terror followed by hope, and more fear and finally death. He said, "Andy, my life is over. How did you keep on going when you lost Mae?"

I didn't really answer him directly. I acknowledged that it has been very difficult, and I still feel deep sadness and sometimes intense depression. But I said, "You will find a way, Lew. God gives us the courage and strength to struggle on, and you will be able to do so. Just don't give up." Then I shared with him that I was writing you these letters and hope to publish them to tell how I am surviving, and I will be sure he gets a copy when I publish. He said he would be eager to get one as have a number of other friends who have also lost the love of their life.

After I hung up, I started thinking about how I am surviving. What is keeping me going? What makes those lonely evenings manageable? There are a number of things: phone conversations, reading, watching TV, writing these letters, dinner out with a friend and/or family member now and then, and probably what I enjoy as much as anything is watching a sporting event on TV, especially baseball. Baseball has always been my favorite sport. It all began from the influence of my father.

You knew Dad well and were fond of him. He was born in Paterson, New Jersey, and was one of eleven. His mother also had two children who died at birth. In a family that large, everyone was counted on to work for the survival of the family. They all found an opportunity for some relaxation in playing games, and the chief one was baseball. They were all avid fans of the Yankees, Giants, and Dodgers—all three teams in New York. Not sure which team Dad preferred, but I do know he liked the Yankees and told me a number of times he met Babe Ruth in person, both in New York and Chicago where he taught school for a while and met my mother. He also played baseball in college and often bragged that he was named Home Run Dixon because in the great rival game with Hope College, he hit the winning home run, making Calvin College the champion. As a young boy, I often looked at his picture in a baseball uniform for Calvin in the annual Prism (yearbook of pictures).

I also played baseball in high school and a little in college, plus American Legion Baseball. Health reasons, involving a misdiagnosis of a heart murmur, prevented me from pursuing it like I desired. I was so disappointed about this. I remember Dad giving me a long encouraging and comforting talk about how there were more important things in life to accomplish beyond baseball. I don't know if I told you this before. I am sure I have because as you told me on a few occasions, "You are baseball nuts." It was particularly so when you had to listen on the car radio as I was trying to pick up a broadcast of the Detroit Tigers game while traveling, and all you could hear was the static. You would say rather disgustingly, "Can you hear anything of that game? It's driving us crazy!"

No longer do I listen on a hard to hear radio. Now I watch games on the large TV. And so, on most lonely evenings, you can find me in that recliner, the one we bought so I could sleep after breaking my shoulder, watching a Tiger game. I have purchased a package that allows me to livestream any major league game on my computer and then mirror it to the large TV. I look forward to watching a game most evenings that I am not otherwise involved or occupied. Through the years, as you know, I enjoyed it. In Pompton Plains, I had that little room in the "slave quarters," which served both as study and lounge to watch games; and in the Poconos, I had the whole loft which became a man cave. Now the living room serves that purpose, and most evenings, I enjoy watching and hoping for the Tigers to win. This year, Detroit has a bad team, and I find myself shutting off a game they are losing. I choose a book to read or search the internet.

Anyway, hon, that is one of the ways I find a bit of enjoyment without you. It helps me survive. Lew Schafer plays the guitar and quite well. He is also a member of a band that has given him pleasure, and I am sure it will continue to do that. Maybe he can focus on his love for music? I am sure he will find a way to survive, but it won't be easy. As much as I love baseball, I would give it all up just to have you back in my life!

Love ya, hon!

Women Friends

—✐—

Dear Mae,

In a previous letter, I mentioned bumping into Gabe and Shiela Rosko in Costco. During our brief conversation, they asked if I had found another woman in my life. I told them no, and they seemed somewhat surprised. Others have also queried me on the same subject. So I feel I want to reflect with you on how I have experienced and feel about women in my life since I lost you.

You were the shining joy of my life and my helpmate. There were times, when like every couple, we had struggles and scuffles. There were times when I felt you didn't understand, and I know you had the same feeling. There was never a time the problems became so dominant that either of us considered any kind of separation. I just always counted on you being there for me, and I figure you felt the same. We talked often about who would die first because we believed "until death do us part." We both figured it would be me to leave first due to all the cancer issues I had confronted, and then you left me suddenly, most unexpectedly in a way we never imagined.

Once I got past the initial shock and life got somewhat back to being somewhat normal, although I doubt if I will ever consider it normal again, I began to ask some questions. Is this the way it will remain? Will I be a single person the rest of my life? Or is there someone out there to be a partner, a companion, maybe even a second spouse? At first, because it was so difficult getting used to having to do all the things you did to make life work, I felt rather convinced that I would have to find someone as a partner. I especially needed someone with whom to converse. There were so many decisions I felt unable to make myself with respect to family, finances, care of our home, celebrations of birthdays, continuing extended family contacts, and especially the care of Candice. I could go on. It all seemed to be overwhelming without you!

I also missed our physical touch, just going to sleep with each other every night and feeling the warmth of your body next to mine. We had a very good life of intimacy. We did enjoy the fun associated with our sexual relationship. We were free and open with our bodies. We could laugh at the physical changes that took place as we grew older. We were always fully open to the other's naked presence. We cared for each other through physical illnesses that demanded being fully attentive to the other's body. For you, there was the renal artery surgery back in our final days in Miami, and of course, giving birth to our daughters. For me, it was the broken shoulder, bouts of cancer, and stem-cell replacement. We cared for each other, cleaned each other up, and encouraged each other the best we could. We helped nurse each other back to health, a tough task at times but one that contributed to the complete openness we enjoyed.

There are many intimate moments that live vividly in my memory. You always made our times of intimacy so much fun. You loved all of life and helped me and many others to enjoy life more fully as well. You had those fun things about how you celebrated ordinary events. I really miss that. We shared this kind of fun and intimacy to the very last days of your life, and I often find myself longing for your hugs and kisses.

Aware of all these various needs, I have reached out to connect with females near my age, mostly widows, a couple divorcées. I feel there is no map to follow and no destination to reach. I don't really know what I want in a relationship with a woman. I know what we had and know it cannot be repeated. I can't help comparing every female I contact with what I remember and know of you. I have come to a conclusion of what I don't want. I enjoy my independence and don't want to give it up. I don't want a relationship that calls for much involvement with another's extended family or that person with mine. I don't want to be seen as a helpless male who needs a female for direction and protection. I want a relationship with someone with whom I can have interesting conversations, animated discussions, and even arguments at times. I would enjoy periodic phone calls, texting, a dinner or lunch together, and opportunities to engage in various activities, movies, and special programs. I just want someone with whom I can feel a warmth and openness even though we may think differently on various issues. If a close relationship develops, I will be open and enjoy it. I am sure you would want this for me, and I would want it for you, as we discussed many times.

It is often frustrating to be alone when you want to be with someone. However, I have seen too many widows or widowers make a decision to form a partnership with someone and let it grow to the point where it becomes a burden, and for some, even a tragic marriage that makes life even more difficult. Fortunately, our daughters seem pleased that I have female friends and affirm me, not like some situations I have known where daughters didn't want fathers to get involved after losing their mother.

There probably is much more I could share with you on this subject, but I leave it here. And my concluding thought is, you were just the best, honey. You had it all, and I have been spoiled. This attitude probably keeps me from giving maximum effort to form a new close relationship. Not sure I would counsel others who have lost their love to think this way. It could make for more loneliness. I guess all this says I am very uncertain about any future partner or close relationship. Just thinking about someone in my life other than you makes me somewhat anxious. I don't think you would have had that problem. You were more able to develop friendships than me. That is a subject for some further reflection. For now, love ya, hon!

Memorial Day

Dear Mae,

It is Memorial Day, always a rather special day for us. I just returned from having a lonely breakfast at a diner. I decided upon waking that I was going out for breakfast even if there was no one to go with me. It just seemed right for the day on which we always did something special to celebrate the beginning of summer and honor all who lived and died. We would think of our parents and extended family and also those who gave their lives in defense of freedom in the service of the country. After serving thirty-two years in the Air Force, we always had a special place in our hearts for those who lost their lives in battles that we hoped would provide peace but never have. I thought of the times we took the kids into New York City to see some event that was honoring the military. I remember the trip we took to the *Intrepid* and am grateful we had and shared those experiences with our children. I also thought of the years we lived in Pompton Plains and marched in the parade and spoke at the memorial service following on the church lawn with the monument. I thought of how Candice took her trumpet and marched with various bands in this part of North Jersey to commemorate the day. So I do feel a bit melancholy and lonely.

Also, I read this piece as part of a daily e-mail, provided by a funeral home that sends this to help people dealing with grief. There is a different quote shared each day.

> The idea of immortality, that like a sea has
> ebbed and flowed in the human heart, with its

countless waves of hope and fear, beating against the shores and rocks of time and fate, was not born of any book, nor of any creed, nor of any religion. It was born of human affection, and it will continue to ebb and flow beneath the mists and clouds of doubt and darkness as long as love kisses the lips of death. It is the rainbow—hope shining upon the tears of grief. (Robert G. Ingersoll)

"Whether or not you believe in a form of eternity, know that your loved one will live forever in your heart and memories." An unknown interesting comment! It is love that keeps you alive in my heart and memory, and it is also God as love that gives me the hope that in some way, we will meet again in a fuller and more complete relationship. In looking over the letters I have written, I think I have been quite clear about the continuing reality of my faith in God. One thing I have not articulated is how my thinking about God has changed. Recently, I reread Nick Wolterstorff's book *Lament for a Son*, as well as his more recent memoir, *A World of Wonder*. What struck me is how he shared that his idea of God has changed because of the loss of his son, but not his faith in God. That is pretty much how I feel. I guess I would go on to say that it has changed and is changing.

A recent book I am reading is *The Sin of Certainty* by Peter Enns. His major theme is that we can't build our faith on correct thinking. Right thinking has been so central to our education in Reformed theology. It is refreshing to read what else he says. At one point he writes,

I point humbly to one of the key pillars (and mysteries!) of the Christian faith, that God enters into human suffering and dies. I'll just leave it at that. If I say more, I'm afraid it will look like I'm trying to explain it. I am amazed and encouraged by those who have lived through these moments of hell on earth and have continued on in the life of faith anyway. They have something to teach people like me: no matter what we think we know, no matter how sure we happen to think we are, suffering is the place where our sense of certainty about God's ways fades like a dream and forces us to consider that what we know may not be as central to our faith as we might think. (Peter Enns, *The Sin of Certainty*, p. 134, HarperOne, Kindle Edition)

Quite often, after sharing with people your loss and then also tell of the death of Candice, they pause in silence and look at me intently and ask, "Do you ever get bitter or angry?"

Most of the time, I respond saying, "Yes." Then I go on to say, "However, I realize bitterness won't help. I need to accept it. Death comes to all." I do feel anger—why did it have to be me who suffered this double loss? However, the thought that sticks is that dying is part of living. None of us can escape it, and my task now is to find the means to live on and use your death to help me become more whole and compassionate. When my mood was not positive as I suffered through the various bouts of cancer, you had a phrase you repeated often, "Your task is to get healed. That is all you have to work on right now."

You were right, and that is my task now as well. I need to find healing for the empty feelings and loneliness, and I am working on it. It is my major task for the remainder of my life here on earth Thank you, hon, for preparing me so well for this task by always challenging me to try to create new hope out of every crisis we faced.

"Most Memorial Days I wore my uniform for the prayers or speeches at the Monument in Pompton Plains and you always looked your best and I was so proud of my wife.

I Have Moved to a New Home

Darling Mae,

As I intimated in the last few letters, I am at that place in life where I am seriously feeling body breakdown and lack of the energy to which I was accustomed. No more golf, reduced walking, diminished swimming! I am at the point where I carry a cane some of the time to provide stability. There are times I feel a bit dizzy and have fallen, and other times when I have almost fallen. I just don't enjoy meal preparation as I did in the past. I began to feel it was time to sell the condo and move on. Within two months of first thinking about it, I made the move to go to Cedar Crest. You know all about the place. We watched it being built during our time in Pompton Plains. We also checked it out before we retired believing one day, we would have to secure an apartment there where all services would be provided. When I served on the hospital board at Chilton, I had a number of meals and meetings there as we negotiated with their leaders about providing health care for their occupants.

Now I am here. I purchased a two-bedroom apartment on the sixth floor facing northeast. This provides a very attractive view. I can see all the way to the Wanaque Reservoir and into the Ramapo mountains. My first couple weeks here were very pleasant, and I met many new people, plus old acquaintances. Then everything changed. The whole world was hit with a deadly virus that caused a great number of deaths in our country and every place. To deal with this condition, quarantines were set up in many places including our complex. We were not permitted to leave our apartments for almost six weeks.

We were required to wear masks when we were able to go out, and the condition of wearing masks has continued for more than a year.

The lack of interpersonal contact on a regular basis has caused loss of memory for many at different degrees. I have been quite affected by it. I took a test recently in which the normal scale of memory for people my age is twenty-seven to thirty. Mine was at twenty-five. It has caused me problems remembering where I have put things and especially people's names. It has made the move less than pleasant.

I have also gone through a procedure called TAVR which is the replacement of my aortic valve by a catheter which was inserted through my groin into the heart. I also received a pacemaker in the same manner so my heart could keep up. It seems to have been very successful, and I am now taking post cardiac therapy to continue the healing process. I consider it most fortunate because Morristown hospital, where it was done, is considered one of the top hospitals in the county for this kind of treatment, and the doctors also have excellent reputations.

There are also some enticing and enriching things that have happened since my move. It has enabled contact with many old friends from Pompton Plains. Also brought Karen, Bruce, and grandkids a lot closer. One of the chaplains here is Tom Larkin. Having worked with him so many years, it is good to be close to him again. There are also some new people with whom I have connected. One person I connected with as a result of moving here is a woman also named Karen, who lives in Ada, Michigan, just outside Grand Rapids. We connected through a podcast I did for the church during the beginning of the response the church made to the virus. The pastors livestreamed a number of times at the beginning of the virus, and Pastor Kathleen asked me to contribute a couple times as well. Sister Jeanne sent one to Karen, and somehow it led to our reconnecting by phone. Ever since, we have talked regularly. You may have remembered meeting her and her mother at my father's viewing. They were members of Dad's last church in Grand Rapids, and during my first year in seminary, we dated.

It has been quite pleasant because we have had some very interesting conversations. Talking with her has brought back a load of good memories about Air Force days and time in seminary. She was married about the same time we were to a lieutenant/colonel in the Army. She spent time living in Japan and also stateside near Washington, DC. She had three children born while they were in the military as two of our girls were born while I was in uniform. Connecting with her not only brought to mind the military experience but being brought up in the Dutch Calvinist tradition, she went to a Christian School, attended the Christian Reformed Church, and since Dad was her pastor, her parents also knew our family.

The most significant connection is that her husband was also killed in an automobile accident as you. The big difference is that they were only married eleven years at the time. She never remarried and raised her three children to become accomplished adults with families. There is much to discuss when we look back at our individual life journeys. Since we did date almost a whole semester, I was interested in why we broke up. I couldn't remember how or when. She figures we were both young at the time and pretty busy with preparation for our careers; she as a nurse and me with all the seminary studies.

Because of all the similarities in our life's journey, we have much to converse. Additionally, we have similar political positions, and during the last election, it was always comforting and challenging to find someone who believed along similar lines and could relate their positions to their faith commitment. I also marvel at Karen's strength of resolve to live a positive life in which she is an example of great hope. She reminds me of Paul's thoughts in 1 Thessalonians 4:13, "Although we grieve we do not do so as those who have no hope." I feel great hurt by my loss of you and still shed tears easily but wish to lead others to discover in the journey of grief a hope that lasts and carries all of us through the worst of times as well as the best.

Writing to you has provided a path for me to get in touch with and express feelings that might have remained hidden and haunted me. I also want to encourage others to be able to share their feelings of loss and grief as a way to discover the peace that God offers those of us who grieve. I know that will not be comfortable for everyone, but even if these letters get some to think and feel more deeply and compassionately about life, it has been worth it. I feel that now it is time to conclude. I have learned much about my needs and those of others sharing these personal feelings with you. I wish I could hear your response, but because we have shared so many things during our years together, I think I know how you would respond to much of it.

It has been excellent therapy to do grieving in this fashion. I have received strength and courage for building positive thoughts. Hopefully I can look forward to a favorable and optimistic future, even at my advanced age. I trust God will guide. Living in a new environment will continue to create new acquaintances and new opportunities. Because we lived in Pompton Plains for so many years, it will reconnect me with old friends who have been so loving and kind to us through the twenty-one years we lived there as a pastor's family.

I have also written to the person who operated the huge vehicle that caused your death. I have thought often of how he must be experiencing life since the accident and want him to know that because love always promotes hope, it is my wish he will experience the forgiving sense of God's love and hope for new life regardless of what he is and has gone through since that fateful day. Because of the wonder of your love and forgiveness of all my failures over the years, I am wishing for him the same love of God's forgiveness and our family's willingness to forgive.

Ever continuing to feel the greatest love for you! God gave us a wonderful life together, ever teaching us that everything may not turn out as we desired, but through it all, the great peace and love of God will find us! Hugs and kisses! Your lover, Andrew

Letter Written and Sent to the Truck Driver Who Caused the Fatal Accident

Dear ——,

I really don't know how to begin this letter. It is something I have been considering for some time and have postponed it out of uncertainty about how to communicate in a manner you will understand. I am the husband of the late Mae Rienstra who was one of the women who died in the accident on October 13, 2014, on Rt. 209 in East Stroudsburg, Pennsylvania. Ever since I learned of the accident and the fact that you were the operator of the truck involved, I have been wondering just how this experience has affected your life.

Having served as an Air Force chaplain and a parish minister in the Reformed Church in America for many years, I have ministered to a great number of people who have been involved in tragic accidents. These incidents cause grief, guilt, remorse, depression, and many other emotional and spiritual conditions in all people affected. As you well understand, my family, consisting of three daughters and their spouses and children, were initially devastated. In working through our grief, all of us were also concerned about how this accident must have changed your life as well.

Although we couldn't help experiencing anger when we discovered some of the details of the accident, we gradually came to the awareness that life can never be fully managed, that there are mistakes that happen at every level. Some are minor, and we all make them. Some more major, and many of us make them. And others are very significant and life changing; some of us make them. This is how we have come to see your involvement in this accident. We are certain it was not an action you intended. Although we will grieve forever, we also feel for you and your family and want to express our empathy.

Growing older, I realize my days on this earth are shrinking, and I have pledged that there is no way I want to leave here without letting you know that I hold no grudge or animosity toward you for what took place. I have talked with my daughters as well about such feelings, and they feel with me. We want you to know that although there is no way we can change the past. We wish for you to go forward knowing that this family forgives you and wishes for you to live with a sense of peace.

If you are able and ever wish to make contact, feel free to do so.

Sincerely,
Andrew Rienstra

Karen's Eulogy at Candice's Funeral

As I sit here thinking on Candice's life, I remember her being the leader of the Rienstra girls. Growing up, she was the one who had us cheering for the Miami Dolphins, playing jokes on our parents, leading our sneaky nighttime runs back and forth from our bedrooms while my parents were sitting right there watching TV. (We later found out that they knew what we were doing the whole time.)

When we were with the extended family, she was the oldest of all the cousins. There again, she was the leader and orchestrated all our missions and adventures like outdoor expeditions to Meijers or swimming in Grandma's lake. She was always fun and exciting to be around.

When she was in elementary school, she was a die-hard athlete who could play any sport as good as the boys. In high school, she was an outstanding basketball and softball player. Not only did she enjoy participating, she loved watching sports, and her room was plastered with Miami Dolphin newspaper articles. She wore her Dolphin jersey religiously.

She was a hard act to follow in high school. She was loved by her teachers and classmates. She was involved in so many activities.

And although she enjoyed everything about life in those days, the thing she loved the most was her music. She would always play her trumpet. In fact, I was so awestruck by her trumpet. I tried playing it myself a few years in school.

Also, she spent a lot of time at our church, working with the technology there to make sounds and music. She would come home and share her recordings with us. Sound was her inspiration. She had an ear for new and different sounds. If you were from another country with a strong accent, she would get engrossed in a conversation with you, and she would pick up your accent. She was so intrigued by the inflections of the voice. No wonder she majored in speech and music in college. Everything she did, she did it with her all. She never was afraid to try and do anything. No fear! Both of us looked up to her and wanted to be just like her.

Unfortunately, while she still held the same passion for life, her illness derailed her. It was difficult to see the change in her. She separated herself from us, and it was like we lost her then. There were some very difficult years, especially for my parents. We still tried to keep her involved in our lives, but she was not willing to join us. Eventually, she found a group home in Boonton with a whole new group of people that she adopted as her new family. They took care of her, and she took care of them. I'm told she helped out a lot of the other clients at the home and also would play her trumpet and keyboard for them. She may not have had a life that was successful by the world's definition, but she did have a successful life by her own definition where she could share her talents with those she loved and cared for.

Candice, we love you so much. We will miss you dearly. This is a very bittersweet ending to your physical life, but I am grateful that you are now free of your illness and can be whole again. As Bev and Dave wrote on their card, "The trumpet shall sound… We shall be changed!"

"As Karen writes, Candice was the leader of her siblings and cousins. she thought up the games, cared about others and always made it fun to be with her."

About the Author

Andrew Rienstra is a retired pastor who served churches in northern New Jersey and Miami, Florida. He was also an Air Force Reserve chaplain, for thirty-two years assigned to numerous bases and assisting with career development programs. He was married to Mae Bangma for fifty-five years prior to her untimely death. Together they led numerous marriage enrichment and parent effectiveness seminars. They were privileged to enjoy three daughters and six grandchildren.

Rienstra considers himself a progressive religious leader who appreciates value in all faith groups and emphasizes love, compassion, and justices as the central themes of his ministry. He graduated from Calvin University and Seminary in Grand Rapids, Michigan, and received a doctor of ministry degree from Princeton Seminary. He has kept physically active, engaging in regular exercise, playing golf, and skiing. Among his many interests are watching sporting events, reading, music, theatre, travel, and spending time with family and friends. Together, he and Mae have journeyed to various places in the Far East and Europe. On one occasion, they traded pulpits and homes with a pastor in Scotland. With their family, they visited forty-eight of the fifty states. Presently the author lives in a retirement facility in Pompton Plains, New Jersey